T0170329

Rural Sociology and the Environment

This volume is one of a series of six studies to be published by Greenwood Press under the auspices of the Rural Sociological Society. Professor James J. Zuiches, of Washington State University, is the series editor. The topics covered by this series include community, natural resources, structure of agriculture, diffusion of innovations, population, and the history and social context of rural sociological research.

RURAL SOCIOLOGY AND THE ENVIRONMENT

DONALD R. FIELD
&
WILLIAM R. BURCH, Jr.

Foreword by
EUGENE A. WILKENING

UNDER THE AUSPICES OF THE
RURAL SOCIOLOGICAL SOCIETY

Social Ecology Press
Middleton ● Wisconsin

Library of Congress Cataloging-in-Publication Data

Field, Donald R.
    Rural sociology and the environment / Donald R. Field and William
R. Burch, Jr. ; forword by Eugene A. Wilkening.
        p.   cm. — (Contributions in sociology, ISSN 0084—9278 ; no.
74)
    "Under the auspices of the Rural Sociological Society."

    Bibliography: p.
    Includes index.
    ISBN 0-941042-11-1
    1. Sociology, Rural. 2. Man—Influence of environment. 3. Human
ecology. 4. Natural resources. I. Burch, William R., 1933—
II. Title. III. Series.
HT 421.F47 1988
307.7'2—dc19   88-15483

British Library Cataloguing in Publication Data is available.

Library of Congress Catalog Card Number: 90-64070
ISBN: 0-941042-11-1
ISSN: 0084-9278

First published in 1988 by Greenwood Press, Inc.

Second edition paperback published 1991
by Social Ecology Press

Social Ecology Press™
P.O. Box 863
Middleton, Wisconsin 53562
Printed in the United States of America

10   9   8   7   6   5   4   3   2   1

Contents

Figures and Table

Figures

Table

Foreword

The study of rural life began in the early part of this century as professors in the land grant colleges and public officials became concerned about the patterns of life in the country and how such patterns were affected by natural as well as social factors. This book is a recognition of the special attention given by rural sociologists and other professionals to natural resources as a basis for understanding rural life, its problems, and opportunities—a focus that has been given renewed emphasis by a Natural Resources Research Group within the Rural Sociological Society.

What follows is a personal statement by two sociologists who were part of the Rural Sociological Society in the beginning and throughout the development of the Natural Resources Research Group's contribution to the study of environment. The first chapter of the book focuses on settlement patterns and the interrelationship of settlement and natural conditions for the production of food and fiber in the early part of the twentieth century. Such studies led to an interest in the people, their institutions, and their services by the early rural sociologists. It began with C. Galpin's *Social Anatomy of a Rural Community* and was followed by studies of locality groups and communities by J. Kolb in Wisconsin, D. Sanderson in New York State, and P. Landis in Washington State. These and related studies became a dominant type of inquiry into changes oc-

curring in agriculture, trade, and services, and how their association affected the size and type of cities and the social
relationships of rural people. A few such as Ray Wakeley in
Illinois and Walter Firey in Massachusetts became concerned
with the nature of land use, soil erosion, and its effect on the
people in the 1930s and 1940s. Then changes in the use of land
and water resources as well as transportation and industrialization led to nationwide studies of the growth and decline of
trade centers supported by the Division of Farm Population
and Rural Life of the U.S. Department of Agriculture.

This volume gives attention to the early literature as a background for more recent concern about man's relationship to the
natural environment in its many forms. With the older ecological rural sociology, the connection was made through the
production process and the way this process connected man and
nature within the context of the basic need to extract a live-
lihood from nature. The authors show how concern for the interrelationship of man and the environment gave rise to the
concern for ecology by the demographers, particularly their use
of census data to illustrate the interaction of population, social
organization, environment, and technology (the POET model
of O. D. Duncan) to explain change in rural life. What was still
lacking was an adequate theory of how these factors interacted
to affect one other.

A new set of problems for rural sociologists developed in the
1970s as the energy crisis and the limitations of water, forests,
and recreational resources called attention to the limits to
growth and development. This recognition led to the environmental movement with its new focus on natural resources. It
was during this period that the authors, D. R. Field and W. R.
Burch, became involved and contributed to the literature relating man to changes in the natural environment. It was also
a period in which F. Cottrell's *Energy and Society*, Dennis
Meadow's *Limits to Growth*, and Paul Ehrlich's *Human Ecology*
began to influence the research and teaching in rural sociology.
Burch's *Daydreams and Nightmares*, in 1971, was one of the
early contributions reflecting the problems of the man-nature
relationship. The authors attempt to tie in the literature of this
period with that of earlier writers such as Carle Zimmerman

in the 1930s and Walter Firey in the 1940s. The combined work expanded the domain of nature in rural sociology although an adequate theoretical basis for doing so was lacking. The authors of this volume provide a framework for relating the changes in nature and man to human organizations and behavior, drawing from a wide range of sources. The biological and physical aspects of social systems are recognized and taken into account by a number of writers, such as B. Catton and R. Dunlap, but have not become integrated into the mainstream research of rural sociologists. Emphasis here is given to the more specific studies of rural sociologists where attention to environmental problems, from wildlands to wetlands and farm to factory, were studied. The limitations of more specialized approaches are appropriately indicated. The authors move toward a much needed holistic approach in the latter part of the book under the heading "Emergence of Nature as a Partner." Here they show how the social systems interact with ecosystems acknowledging both the positive and the negative effects each has on the other. They draw from the anthropologists and from the wider range of literature to understand the relationship of the non-human environment to human relationships of all types. Their concern is how human relationship to the natural environment differs in different countries, regions, and communities, and how these differences affect human relationships themselves. It is here that they deal with the effect of rural area development and changes, including transportation, housing, water impoundment, and mining, on social relationships. It is the interaction of the ecological and social systems that has become most important to an understanding of human-nature relations. Such thinking gives support for social and environmental impact studies of programs and projects of all types. As the authors indicate, environmental sociology is "a problem focus, not a theoretical orientation." They suggest the need for drawing from a wide range of knowledge in both the natural and social areas to understand and arrive at sustainable ecological and social systems.

Eugene A. Wilkening

Rural Sociology and the Environment

Preface

The literature of rural sociology makes it clear that sociologists who focused on social behavior, rural family life, rural communities, and the study of primary enterprises such as agriculture and forestry were fundamentally concerned with the relationship of a rural people to their environment.

This monograph will demonstrate that contributions of rural sociologists to environmental sociology have been consistent and significant. It is not our intention to suggest that rural sociologists were or are natural resource sociologists. Some were and are. Some not. Nor do we suggest rural sociologists were or are social ecologists. Some were and are. Some not. But there are threads of ecological awareness among many students of rural society from the beginnings of our discipline. These ideas are reflected in an understanding of human adaptation to natural resource systems and appear in theoretical explanations of rural community persistence, growth and decline, the structure of agriculture, and social integration of rural society.

The monograph also represents our attempt to highlight the contributions of rural sociology to the ongoing theoretical and methodological development of natural resource sociology. This is because the Rural Sociological Society (RSS) and its Natural Resources Research Group (NRRG) have provided an organizational environment that has given legitimacy to those schol-

ars who have worked outside of conventional sociological paradigms and venues. We highlight the work of those sociological
pioneers. The first are those sociological *mavericks* trained in
rural sociology who dared to remember that rural sociology is
the study of social behavior, natural resources, and the environment. The second group is composed of those *explorers*
trained in disciplines such as general sociology, social psychology, and anthropology who brought to their studies of the
environment theoretical paradigms derived elsewhere, expanding and enriching rural sociological thought. The third
group comprises those *hybrids* trained in a resource-oriented
program or school such as forestry, marine studies, and recreation and parks (often with a biological background) who
adopted social science theory and methods in order to understand resource management issues and explain resource conflicts.

Thus, natural resource sociologists are an eclectic group of
scholars representing a variety of theoretical perspectives on
social behavior and natural resources. A common focus for
many, however, is that knowledge of the process and structure
in a social-biological system is critical to understanding the
persistence and change of rural social institutions, rural values, and adaptive mechanisms rural inhabitants employ to survive on the land, in the forests, and on the seas.

Our intent also is to stress the two-way flow of ideas and
applications between natural resource issues and rural sociology. On the one hand, the Rural Sociological Society first,
and then later the NRRG have provided a respectable forum
for unexpected, unpopular, and unpredictable ideas about humankind and the environment that have contributed to broader
understanding of rural life. On the other hand, this creative
milieu has been responsible for continuity, conceptualization,
and application of sociological thought to resource management
issues.

With regard to continuity, the RSS has served as a base for
discussion of sociological concerns about differences in social
organization in rural (low density) and urban (high density)
residential environments, the relationship of farm size and distribution to rural trade center growth and decline, the asso-

ciation of generalized versus specialized farm enterprises to ecological diversity both human and biological, the relationship of soil erosion and droughts to community stability, the interplay of human values and organization associated with the primary production process, and the resulting moral economy and patterns of society's social integration.

The RSS has supported a base of conceptualization in which nature in both its broadest and narrowest sense (from the heavens to microbes) has been part of an explanation about the social regularities of behavior. The variables of distance, of seasons, of pests, and of genetic strains of plants and animals have all been examined for their role in shaping social regularities of households and communities. The NRRG has served as a respectable forum for wildcard ideas. Attempts to speak the unspeakable have been aired—cross-species comparisons, the importance of natural resources in determining social structure, the thrust of biology over culture, and the crucial value of leisure over work.

The renewed thrust of applied science issues in the RSS in some respects has been rekindled by natural resource issues and the interest by the NRRG to foster communication between scientist, practitioner, and professional resource manager. The group's annual meetings have served as a place for the exchange of ideas and application strategies for both managers and applied social scientists from a mixture of disciplines. These are people who desired to find behavioral solutions to human-caused forest fires, forest recreation patterns, social conflicts in nature, human dimensions in wildlife, social impact assessment, discussions of the social organization of resource management organizations, and most recently, the science of "applied science." In fact, the application of sociological theory and method to practice on contemporary resource management issues is ongoing in the Natural Resources Research Group. The location of nuclear waste dumps, sitings of MX missiles— these are rural society issues that affect agriculture, forestry, parks, and rural lifestyle; and certainly genetic research in agriculture has implications for farm structure, rural institutions, and rural environments.

The rural sociological academic heritage would not be fully

noted without a word about the influence of the society and its Natural Resources Research Group on the organization of research and discussion of society-environment relations. RSS members helped spawn the environmental sociology group within the American Sociological Association and were instrumental in the initiation of sessions on the environment held as part of the annual meetings of the Society for the Study of Social Problems (SSSP). More recently, leaders of the NRRG have assumed positions of leadership within the Rural Sociological Society. Two past chairs of the NRRG have been elected vice presidents of the parent society.

Finally, we would be remiss if we failed to note the academic home for much of the early work on rural sociology and the environment. The agricultural experiment station (AES) has been instrumental at times in support for much of the research on environmental issues conducted by rural sociologists. Many of the classic studies on rural sociology and the environment are experiment station bulletins sponsored by research funds provided by AES within a college of agriculture. Many of the contemporary studies published in rural sociology are also funded in part by agricultural experiment stations. Support for such work, however, has been uneven over the past fifty years. More recently, agricultural administrations have emphasized research on the production process at the expense of a more holistic understanding of organization of the farm enterprise as an agricultural system, genetic research on plant and animal species at the expense of knowledge about the people who tend the flocks and cultivate the fields as a human resource system, and increased emphasis on single species animal and plant production yields at the expense of increased knowledge about contemporary farm families and diverse ecological patterns of farming and rural communities. As J. L. Hypes noted in 1944 when attempting to solve soil erosion problems, once attention is directed to the human resource in concert with the biological question, solutions will be found. After all Hypes (1944:364) noted, "soil erosion is in essence human erosion. One cannot be solved without the other." The agricultural experiment stations should once again examine closely the role of rural people and their institutions within a "rural ecology" framework.

A monograph on rural sociology and the environment is indeed appropriate as we celebrate the fiftieth anniversary of the Rural Sociological Society. Our is a proud heritage. The legacy of the RSS to natural resource sociology is long and enduring. Our volume here does not reflect all that has transpired about the environment within the RSS. For example, the excellent and emerging work by rural sociologists on the sociology of fisheries and international social forestry is not systematically examined in the present volume. And certainly we do not attempt to describe the entire field of environmental sociology or even the general field of natural resource sociology. *Rather, the perspective drawn here is our personal perception and interpretation reflecting our participation in the rich triple tradition of agricultural sociology, human ecology, and environmental sociology.* We highlight the knowledge that has been exchanged within the parent society and the NRRG about social behavior and natural resource systems.

Two questions one always asks when writing a monograph such as this are What have we learned and contributed to a body of knowledge? and, perhaps equally important, What have we contributed in applying such knowledge to an understanding of how primary production systems operate? W. Firey (1978) has urged natural resource sociologists to reflect on their legacy and suggested that we have not taken credit for what we have accomplished. D. R. Field and D. R. Johnson (1985) likewise have recently documented the work of some unknown or infrequently cited work contributing to the natural resource field, suggesting we are ignoring some of our heritage. Perhaps this monograph can help us reclaim and build on this record of accomplishment.

REFERENCES

Field, Donald R., and Darryll R. Johnson. 1985. "Rural communities and natural resources: let's not forget the pioneers." In *Rural Sociologists at Work*, ed. B. Bealer, 133–141. University Park, Pennsylvania: The Pennsylvania State University, M. E. John Memorial Lecture Series Fund.

Firey, Walter. 1978. "Some contributions of sociology to the study of natural resources." In Challenges of Societies in Transition, ed. M. Barnabas, S. K. Hullie, and P. S. Jacob, 162–174. New Delhi, India: Macmillan.

Hypes, J. L. 1944. "The social implications of soil erosion." *Rural Sociology* 9:364–376.

Acknowledgments

Several organizations have supported the preparation of this monograph. The Western Rural Development Center along with the College of Forestry at Oregon State University and School of Forestry and Environmental Studies at Yale University maintain research interests in the interaction of social and biological systems, the interdependency of forestry and agriculture, and in particular the impact of resource cycles on resource-dependent communities. They see this volume as a contribution to those ends. The National Park Service (NPS), responsible for the protection of this nation's unique natural and cultural resources, recognizes the interaction effect of parks and their sociobiological regions. Because many parks and preserves are located in rural areas, the service seeks understanding of the resource management strategies of other landholders (private and public) whose management practices (agriculture, forestry, and mining) occur adjacent to park boundaries influencing the social and biological ecosystem processes within parks. They likewise see the volume as useful to bringing such issues to attention of park managers and wardens throughout the world.

Several Rural Sociological Society members have critiqued the monograph during various stages of preparation. Jim Zuiches provided advice and counsel on organization and content, Bob Bealer reviewed and critiqued the monograph at the

1986 RSS meetings in Salt Lake City, Pete Nowak, Neil Cheek, and Eugene Wilkening offered constructive suggestions on the monograph along the way. We are grateful to Ram Guha whose insights and timely inspiration have raised us above provincialism. Jean Matthews, NPS science writer, provided editorial polish to a series of sociological thoughts.

Don Field would especially like to thank the National Park Service for their support of his sociological research program during the past eighteen years. This manuscript was written while Don served as Senior Scientist in the National Park Service, Cooperative Park Studies Unit at Oregon State University. The Department of Forest Recreation at OSU, the host department for NPS Social Science Research, likewise provided clerical assistance in the preparation of this manuscript.

Introduction: Ecological Visions of Nature in Rural Sociology

Rural sociologists have established a scholarly tradition of studies dealing with humankind and the environment. Rural sociologists have for some time been intrigued about how men and women farm the land, mine the earth, and harvest the forests and the seas. This interest is a thread of continuity that pervades the discipline to the present.

In particular, these sociologists have been interested in the social relationships rural people establish to enhance successful adaptation to the environment, where the environment or natural resource system constrains or limits the kind and extent of social relations possible. Rural sociologists also have been interested in the institutions rural people create as well as individual shelters and communities to harness what otherwise might be considered a hostile physical environment. Such institutions provide the organization for production and transport of raw materials to market, the services necessary to sustain a human population on the land and to transfer natural resource proprietorship from one generation to another.

The intellectual curiosity about life in rural America is guided by both social and biological interrelationships. The life of the farmer is guided by the seasons of the year (biological cycles) as are others whose living comes from the land, forest, and sea. The central imperative of human existence is that it is intertwined with the life cycle of plant and animal species.

This is the rural landscape documented by our founders. They recognized the inextricable bond between culture and nature. Natural resources after all are a product of society and the peculiar cultural interpretation of biophysical conditions a society encounters.

This, however, is not to suggest that early rural sociologists were environmental sociologists. Their orientation toward natural resources was couched in the context of rural social problems, where often natural resources were simply viewed as an instrument of rural development. To rural people, the land, the forest, water, and subsurface minerals were a resource to clear, harness, and capture to enhance living conditions in remote areas. Rural sociologists described this orientation to resources as well as the consequences of resource exploitation for human welfare.

It would likewise be an overgeneralization to suggest that the early rural sociologists were all ecologists, but their perspectives and units of analyses were clearly ecological, and were embodied in a view of the rural community and farming as a system. Our perspective today in natural resource sociology is that those institutions and communities created by human effort are also components of the ecosystem. Communities are dynamic; they respond to and alter the resource base on which life depends. In the words of W. S. Saint and E. W. Coward (1977:735) "natural processes and social processes are seen as intertwined." This was very much the view of many early rural sociologists.

ECOLOGICAL ORIGINS IN RURAL SOCIOLOGY

G. A. Theodorson, in noting European studies of spatial relations, suggests that "the study of spatial distribution of interrelated social variables has been an important aspect of human ecology" (1982:3). The mapping of social phenomena juxtaposed on land forms, soils, habitats, river systems, and the like was a popular format to display the type and distribution of social relations being described. Rural sociologists such as C. J. Galpin (1915) employed mapping techniques to describe the social and economic relations of farm families to nearby trade centers. D. Sanderson (1933) did the same thing for a New York county. J. H. Kolb (1921) used spatial mapping in describing the location and distribution of neighborhoods and neighborhood church affiliations. T. Lynn Smith (1933) and Lowry Nelson (1952) employed similar techniques to analyze differences in social interaction among farm families associated with farm settlement patterns in Louisiana and in Utah.

Social mapping was a convenient way to describe the elements of a system, the boundaries of units under analysis, the interrelations of systems' components, and a means of tracking change. J. H. Kolb and R. A. Polson (1933) thus described the growth and decline of trade centers and identified factors associated with population change. Social mapping was utilized by them to document expansion of trade center regions, the ensuing dominance, and, overall, the interdependency of economic activities among centers. C. C. Zimmerman (1930) employed mapping techniques to describe trade center competition and change among types of trade centers in Minnesota; D. Chittick (1955), a quarter of a century later, documented the distribution in number of trade centers by population size over time. Interest in spatial analysis of behavior continues today (G. L. Young, 1974). R. G. Lee (1973) and G. E. Machlis (1975) have employed social mapping in national parks as a way to document visitor distribution and concentration points. B. W. Ilberg (1985) delineates the spatial structure of agriculture in association with various social and economic factors. Current work on computerized geographical information systems (GIS) utilizes mapping techniques to document social and biological interactions, and J. Baldwin (1967), a sociologist, has employed a similar technique to document migration patterns and family territoriality of squirrel monkeys in Central America.

By the mid-1930s, however, social mapping of rural behavior had given way to a more formal (classical ecological) explanation of behavior and resource relationships. Classical ecology emphasized demographic and aggregate measures of populations associated with space, that is, quantitative indicators of human populations at the community or a structural level of analysis. A. P. Vayda and R. A. Rappaport (1976:22) put the matter this way.

> The units important to ecologists are populations (groups of organisms living within a given area and belonging to the same species or variety), communities (all of the populations within a given area), and ecosystems (either individual organisms, populations, or communities, together with their nonliving environments).

Most of the early rural sociologists examined similar units of analysis but with special indicator measures derived from the agriculture production process. In contemporary debates, J. A. Ashby (1982) and the resulting discussion, C. D. Gartell (1983) and Ashby (1985), remind us of the centrality of the agricultural production process and rural ecology.

The genesis of the field was, however, in the desire to meet and combat forces depleting the quality of life in rural America. It is not surprising that attention was placed on economic activities. This institutional area provided the most reliable data to describe social interrelationships of town and farm populations and to explain changes in the social organization of communities. Dun and Bradstreet was a favorite data source to document the number and kinds of business establishments in the rural community. Such indicators helped to develop the notion of a hierarchy of trade centers, correlated with population size and regional influence. The idea of trade center dominance was elaborated and probed by pioneers in rural sociology through various bulletin publications (Galpin, 1915; Lively, 1932; Sanderson, 1933; Anderson, 1953).

Kolb included a discussion of topography and soils in his examination of the formation and distribution of primary groups. A soils map was superimposed on a geographic depiction of social group patterns. Kolb (1921:18) stated that "even casual observation indicates a real relationship between these rural population groupings and the contour of the country, especially when taken along with the original vegetation map." Similarly, P. H. Landis (1933:30), in describing the growth and decline of population in South Dakota rural communities, noted "population increase correlates with the prolonged period of high moisture, whereas the period of decline began during the long drought period." A table is presented on annual precipitation covering the period 1890 to 1935 to support this conclusion.

W. G. Mather, Jr., et al. (1934), discussed the joint effect of economic conditions and soils in the emergence of a new social organization of agriculture affecting both community and region in Waterville, New York. Hop production here was a key agricultural product during the 1880s but began to decline during the latter part of the nineteenth century. Changing soil conditions and price fluctuations were correlated to document the shift in the social organization of local agriculture. Pounds of hops produced was a key resource variable used. The bulletin, likewise, is a story about human settlement, competition, and succession as the authors draw attention to the ebb and flow of commerce and resulting compositional change in population comprising this trade center area.

Chittick (1955), as a final example, described the settlement patterns and distribution of communities in South Dakota from 1901 to 1951 and concluded that type of soil, as well as rainfall, influenced settlement patterns, the nature of farming practices, and the social organization of rural South Dakota.

Human ecosystems are defined by the interaction of population, social organization, and technology in response to a set of environmental conditions (Duncan, 1964). A. H. Hawley (1950:73) writes, "human ecology, which is also interested in the relations of man to his geographic environment, focuses its attention upon the human interdependencies that develop in the action and reaction of a population to its habitat."

Indeed, the parameters identified by contemporary human ecologists (Young, 1974) are very consistent with many of the theoretical frameworks used by early rural sociologists to understand the organization of rural society. In one way or another Ashby (1985), S. H. Murdock (1979), L. Perez (1979), R. E. Dunlap and K. E. Martin (1983), D. E. Albrecht and Murdock (1984), and others draw attention to the rural ecosystem and thereby contribute to the continuity of ecological thought in rural sociology.

AMPLIFYING THE ECOLOGICAL CONNECTIONS

We believe that the thread that binds the study of rural inhabitants and their environment yesterday and today is social ecology. We suggest that there have been three ecological visions within rural sociology over the past fifty years where human and non-human variables have been jointly addressed to explain social behavior and the environment (Figure 1).

The first vision is *dominion over nature for food and fiber*. During the period 1900–1950, focus of attention by rural sociologists was on description of the interactions within and between farm families, farming communities, and agricultural regions as rural people struggled to settle and harness the land. It was a period when the chronicler of rural life documented the association between farming practices and soil erosion, human adaptation to drought, and the influences of topography and rainfall on settlement patterns and farming systems, but the actual story centers on the agricultural production process, the farmer, and the village trade center that arose to serve them. The farm-trade center mutual dependency was viewed as a human resource system. The detailed discussions of the factors associated with trade center dominance and competition among village centers in time and space represent an ecological awareness of change in the human resource system and an evolving rural social world.

The second period (1950–1975) had its most active time in the 1960s when environmental crises seemed more crucial than declining communities. We call the period *expanding the domain of nature*. It was a time when threats to nature were dominant and the limits of nature exposed, but most importantly a variety of analytical studies of the environment emerged and non-human variables were defined and incorporated into social analysis. It was a period of breadth as well as specialization in environmental studies and a corresponding decline of studies in primary production processes, such as agriculture and forestry. Studies of leisure, wilderness, and the environmental movement fostered new means for measuring

Figure 1
Visions of Nature as Represented by Theoretical Research Clusters in Rural Sociology

I. DOMINION OVER NATURE

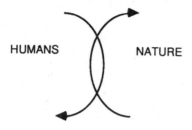

II. EXPANDING THE DOMAIN OF NATURE

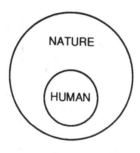

III. NATURE AS A PARTNER

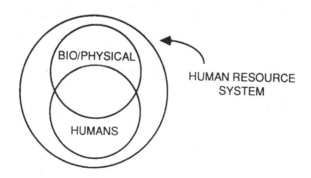

non-human variables. It was in many ways a necessary period
to strengthen our vision of the limiting nature of nature.

The final vision we call *nature as a partner*. It is a period of
renewed ecological thought within rural sociology and other
behavioral sciences. In many ways it is a futuristic period only
now unfolding. It is a period where students of rural society
are integrating what we have learned from the first two periods
into a more holistic and sophisticated picture of human resource ecosystems. Agriculture—like forestry, fisheries, mining, tourism, and the protection of natural resources—can no
longer arise as a resource policy in isolation independent of the
other potential uses of resources. Forestry at the expense of
agriculture, or agriculture at the expense of fisheries, or any
primary resource production process at the expense of resource
protection ignores the system relationships that exist. Conversely, few parks and preserves are of sufficient size to accommodate the protection of a given species within their bounds.
Such enclaves are dependent on the resource management
practices about them to achieve their goal.

The twenty-first-century forester, farmer, government war-
den, and park manager will need to recognize the interdependence of each of their forms of natural resource
management with the others. To succeed, resource management will be considered at a minimum in an ecology system
context, where the totality of resource development, conservation, and protection is considered simultaneously. Competition for resources will give way to cooperative management
strategies, where nature is interpreted as a partner in human
affairs.

The chapters to follow are organized around these visions.
Yet within respective chapters two equally important themes
are addressed. The first is a historical picture of how human
resource relationships have been studied by rural sociologists;
the second is the transformation in the conceptualization of the
human-resource relationship over time and within the disciplinary framework of rural natural resource sociology. Inter-
woven in all the chapters is the "moral imperative" of rural
sociology. The desire to solve real world problems, such as the
concern for the farmer and farm family, the reduction of rural

poverty, elimination of inequities in the distribution of wealth and government services to rural inhabitants, and the conservation and protection of unique resources throughout the world underlie many of the research issues being addressed. Rural sociology is after all a scholarly tradition with a humanistic imperative.

REFERENCES

Albrecht, Don E., and Steve H. Murdock. 1984. "Toward a human ecological perspective on part-time farming." *Rural Sociology* 49:389–411.

Anderson, W. A. 1953. *Social Change in a Central New York Rural Community.* Ithaca, New York: Cornell University Agricultural Experiment Station Bulletin No. 907.

Ashby, Jacqueline A. 1982. "Technology and ecology: implications for innovation research in peasant agriculture." *Rural Sociology* 47:234–250.

Ashby, Jacqueline A. 1985. "The social ecology of soil erosion in a Columbian farming system." *Rural Sociology* 50:377–396.

Baldwin, John D. 1967. "A study of the social behavior of a semi free-ranging colony of squirrel monkeys." Ph.D. dissertation, Johns Hopkins University.

Bertrand, Alvin. 1951. *Agricultural Mechanization and Social Change in Rural Louisiana.* Baton Rouge: Louisiana State University Agricultural Experiment Station Bulletin No. 458.

Bradshaw, Ted K., and Edward J. Blakely. 1971. *Rural Communities in Advanced Industrial Society: Development and Developers.* New York: Praeger.

Chittick, Douglas. 1955. *Growth and Decline of South Dakota Trade Centers 1901–1951.* Brookings: South Dakota State University Agricultural Experiment Station Bulletin No. 448.

Duncan, Otis Dudley. 1964. "Social organization and the ecosystem." In *Handbook of Modern Sociology,* ed. Robert Faris, 36–82. New York: Rand McNally.

Dunlap, Riley E., and Kenneth E. Martin. 1983. "Bringing environment into the study of agriculture: observations and suggestions regarding the sociology of agriculture." *Rural Sociology* 48:201–218.

Friedland, William H. 1982. "The end of rural society and the future of rural sociology." *Rural Sociology* 47:489–608.

Galpin, C. J. 1915. *The Social Anatomy of an Agricultural Community.*

Madison: University of Wisconsin Agricultural Experiment
Station Bulletin No. 34.

Gartell, C. David. 1983. "The social ecology of innovation: a comment
to Ashby." *Rural Sociology* 48:661–666.

Hassinger, Edward. 1956. "Factors associated with population
changes in agricultural trade centers of southern Minnesota
1940–1950." Ph.D. dissertation, University of Minnesota, Minneapolis.

Hawley, Amos H. 1950. *Human Ecology: A Theory of Community
Structure.* New York: The Ronald Press Co.

Ilberg, Brian W. 1985. *Agricultural Geography: A Social and Economic Analysis.* New York: Oxford University Press.

Kolb, J. H. 1921. *Rural Primary Groups: A Study of Agricultural
Neighborhoods.* Madison: University of Wisconsin Agricultural
Experiment Station Bulletin No. 51.

Kolb, J. H., and R. A. Polson. 1933. *Trends in Town-Country Relations.* Madison: University of Wisconsin Agricultural Experiment Station Bulletin No. 117.

Landis, Paul H. 1933. *The Growth and Decline of South Dakota Trade
Centers 1901–1933.* Brookings: South Dakota State University
Agricultural Experiment Station Bulletin No. 279.

Landis, Paul H. 1938. *Washington Farm Trade Centers 1900–1935.*
Pullman: Washington State University Agricultural Experiment Station Bulletin No. 360.

Lee, Robert G. 1973. "Social organization and spatial behavior in
outdoor recreation." Ph.D. thesis, University of California,
Berkeley.

Lively, C. E. 1932. *Growth and Decline of Farm Trade Centers in
Minnesota 1905–1930.* St. Paul: University of Minnesota Agricultural Experiment Station Bulletin No. 287.

Loomis, Charles P. 1983. "In memory of Carle C. Zimmerman." *The
Rural Sociologist* 3:289–290.

Machlis, Gary E. 1975. "Families in parks: an analysis of family organization in a leisure setting." M.S. thesis, University of
Washington, Seattle.

Mather, W. G., Jr., T. H. Townsend, and Dwight Sanderson. 1934. *A
Study of Rural Community Development in Waterville, New
York.* Ithaca, New York: Cornell University Agricultural Ex-
periment Station Bulletin No. 608.

Murdock, Steve H. 1979. "The potential role of the ecological framework in impact analysis." *Rural Sociology* 44:543–565.

Nelson, Lowry. 1952. *The Mormon Village.* Salt Lake City: University
of Utah Press.

Perez, Lisandro. 1979. "The human ecology of rural areas: an appraisal of a field of study with suggestions for a synthesis." *Rural Sociology* 44:584–601.

Saint, William S., and E. Walter Coward, Jr. 1977. "Agriculture and behavioral science: emerging orientations. *Science* 197:733–737.

Sanderson, Dwight. 1933. *Social and Economic Areas of Broome County, New York*. Ithaca, New York: Cornell University Agricultural Experiment Station Bulletin No. 559.

Smith, T. Lynn. 1933. *Farm Trade Centers in Louisiana*. Baton Rouge: Louisiana Agricultural Experiment Station Bulletin No. 234.

Smith, T. Lynn. 1953. *The Sociology of Rural Life*, 3rd ed. New York: Harper and Brothers.

Summers, Gene F., and Arne Selvik. 1979. *Nonmetropolitan Industrial Growth and Community Change*. Lexington, Massachusetts: D.C. Heath & Co.

Taylor, Carl C., et al. 1955. *Rural Life in the United States*. New York: A. A. Knopf.

Theodorson, George A. 1982. *Urban Patterns: Studies in Human Ecology*. University Park: The Pennsylvania State University Press.

Vayda, A. P., and R. A. Rappaport. 1976. "Ecology, cultural and noncultural." In *Human Ecology: Environmental Approach*, ed. P. J. Richerson and J. McEvoy III. North Scituate, Massachusetts: Duxbury Press.

Young, Gerald L. 1974. "Human ecology as an interdisciplinary concept: a critical inquiry." In *Advances in Ecological Research*, ed. A. MacFadyen, 2–88. New York: Academic Press Inc.

Zimmerman, Carle C. 1930. *Farm Trade Centers in Minnesota, 1905–1929*. St. Paul: University of Minnesota Agricultural Experiment Station Bulletin No. 269.

1

The Domination of Nature for Food and Fiber

By 1900, westward expansion in the United States was complete. The conquest or taming of nature for human settlement and occupation had been established. Yet serious social problems in rural America persisted. The depression of the 1890s was not yet merely a memory. Farm income was low, in parts of the country farm tenancy was in chaos, settlement of the west was hindered by drought, and soil erosion on many established farms reduced productivity and affected community stability. Rural migration to the city disrupted the institutions of the neighborhood, church, and school, and the maladjustment of rural residents to city life was noted.

President Theodore Roosevelt, in 1908, appointed a commission to study, interpret, and propose solutions to the social problems in rural America. The barriers to an improved quality of life for rural residents was in part the inability to sustain normal social relations due to time and distance associated with occupancy of the land, the failure of social institutions to provide the necessary human services in the face of spatial barriers, climatological factors, and the failure of particular strains of plant species developed elsewhere to flourish in new habitats.

The formal study of rural life began in response to these social problems. The domination of nature for food and fiber provided the orientation or focus for examining rural life and providing recommendations for an improved quality of life. Domination is employed here in two ways. First, to note the singularity of purpose of rural inhabitants to clear the land for farming or mining with little concern for the interaction effect of agriculture to forestry, wildlife, watershed, management, etc. And second, domination in terms of exploiting the resource with little regard for sustained agriculture practices (i.e., prevention of soil erosion, matching appropriate agricultural practices with soil types, etc.). The academic specialty that was to become rural sociology attempted to document the effects of human actions on the land for rural families, neighborhoods, and communities by instituting a series of descriptive studies of farm-trade center relations, studies of rural institutions such as the rural church and the practice of farming itself. Many of these studies clarified our understanding of the interrelationships of people and their environment and the consequences of attempting to dominate nature.

The chapter proceeds in the following manner. First, those studies that described specific social relationships in conjunction with a change in the biophysical environment are reviewed. Second, a macroview of rural social organization and the environment is discussed through the concept of a natural resource system. Here are reviewed farm-trade center studies that attempt to document change in farm community-land relations. Finally the examples of work from this period on agricultural patterns and rural people are recast in terms of their implication for social impact assessment. Recall that much of the rural sociologists' charge was to understand rural human behavior in a dynamic and evolving rural society.

LIVING ON THE LAND: BIOLOGICAL IMPERATIVES

Natural resource domination, and consequences for personal well-being and community stability, was noted early on as a major rural social problem. Some of the first studies on farming practices focused on the effect of soil erosion on personal and community well-being. For example, R. E. Wakeley (1936) in the first issue of *Rural Sociology* draws attention to the social and economic effects of soil erosion. He suggests in this research note that soil erosion, and thus loss of farm productivity, leads to farm tenancy disruption and town center decay. By disruption, Wakeley observes that on farms where soil erosion is a problem, the occupants of the land tended to be renters not land owners. He leaves us to draw a conclusion as to whether renters or owners have more personal commitment to maintaining soil fertility.

Others, however, are more specific. O. R. Johnson and W. E. Foard (1914) suggested that the existing system of land tenure was undesirable, first because it encourages tenants to become shiftless, second because it depletes the soil, and third because it is detrimental to improvement of rural social conditions. The authors conclude that a person who intends to remain on the land for only a short time pays little attention to soil conservation practices. P. E. Brown (1914:89) echoes this view when he suggests "much of the agricultural land in this country instead of being farmed is being mined." Profit motive associated with a single crop blinds the farmer to the injury he is doing to the soil. Short-term gains (dominion) in other words, are disruptive to a productive farm enterprise and thus long-term personal well-being and community stability are affected (continuity).

Students of soils and culture were far reaching in their measures of association. Soil erosion and soil type were in part indicators of not only tenancy but class structure, wealth, farm size, and poverty. The relationship of status and tenancy was extensively covered. In general, on farms where soil erosion is less, the farmers are of a higher status, able to pay higher wages and benefit from higher crop yields. Similarly higher status farmers occupy better farmlands, tend to produce crops more compatible with the soils, and are involved in more conservation practices. Conversely on farms with high soil erosion, there are more renters than resident owners, the soils are of a poor quality, and the soils in general often are not suited for the type of agriculture practiced. One author suggested that soils (soil type and erosion condition) are a measure of personal wealth and could be a measure of community standard of living, used by real estate appraisers to establish fair market value of a farm. Soil erosion likewise has been linked, implicitly and explicitly, to participation in community affairs where renters demonstrate less involvement in community activities.

The relationship of soil erosion and community stability did not go unnoticed. Implied in several articles is the point that where there is high soil erosion on farms, individual effort is focused on producing a living by exploiting the soil and little human energy remains to contribute to the collectivity, such as maintaining community institutions. A. H. Benton (1918), for example, concludes that in communities where tenancy has developed, soil fertility is being more rapidly depleted, farm and civic improvements are greatly retarded, and the social life of the community is not satisfactory. R. Schickele, et al. (1935:194–195) summarize what many students of soil erosion and farming practices said. "Erosion means more than the mere washing away of the fertile top soils on farms. It means, if it is not checked, the decline of communities with all their schools, churches and other institutions, in addition to ruin of the farm." Writers such as Warren Wilson (1912) capture the moral obligation of sound land management in the portrayal of the evolution of farming as a series of stages from pioneer, to exploiter, to husbandman. In an ideal rural world, issues of domination of the land, natural resource depletion, and exploiting nature for immediate gain would diminish as an agricultural community of husbandmen occupied the countryside. In this later stage, man and nature would blend together.

T. S. Buie (1944) provides a quantitative verification for this contention in his study of the relationship of land and the church. Buie plotted the soil conditions around 222 rural churches. He then grouped the churches into three categories based on soil conditions. His categories were "high soil erosion," "medium soil erosion," and "low soil erosion." The author next asked the question Is farm family participation in the rural church associated with soil erosion condition about the church? His analysis clearly indicates that total membership in the rural church and financial contribution to pastor salaries are highest in those churches where the land around them demonstrated the least amount of soil erosion. There was little difference, however, in actual attendance and participation among parishioners in the various churches.

But in the true applied science tradition, students of soils and culture drew from their work recommendations for maintaining soil fertility and stability of rural society. Two generalizations might be stated. The first is recognizing the appropriateness of a given crop with its associated soil structure and topography. Numerous writers who studied soils and the rural social condition concluded that use of legumes, construction of holding ponds and shelter belts, crop rotation involving a mixture of species, and matching the most appropriate crop with soils were fundamental practices for sustaining the soil. In addition, Smith, et al. (1948) describe a "cropping system" both in terms of plant species and rotation as a process for improving soil conditions on the farm and in the locale.

The second generalization concerns developing an inventory of soils to better match farming systems with soils for a state or region. L. A. Davidson (1943) states the many differences in fertility, texture, elevation, slope, and drainage of soils makes it advisable to vary the management for distinctly different soil types. In writing about the diversity of farming patterns in New York State, R. A. Mordoff (1925) recognized the interplay of temperature and rainfall on agriculture production. In some sections, temperature and length of growing season determine the limits of growth for certain crops; in other sections, rainfall is the dominating influence; and in still others, sunshine is most important. Thus the co-determining influence of soils, topography, and climate on farm productivity was understood. The research community recommended an inventory of soils such that the most compatible use in terms of both productivity and long-term conservation could be determined. This inventory and associated maps would be a guide to farm operators seeking information about the best farming practices for a given region and would help agriculture advisers understand the concept of farming regions, such as dairy, cotton, corn, and wheat, where they could compare a variety of human factors associated with such regions—population structure, community structure, farm size, farm income, tenancy, etc. Inventories likewise would allow for monitoring change in the biological system where crop response (bushels per acre, animals produced, stumpage value, etc.) could become indicators of soil fertility and in general, indicators of biophysical system response to agricultural practices.

J. M. Gillette (1949) attempted to delineate agricultural regions by combining biophysical characteristics and culture of farming into a single variable. He proposed crop response as an indicator of geocultural regionalism. This single measure proved to be an ineffective indicator of the complex biophysical and cultural attributes associated with farming. Nevertheless, the recognition of a regional system as a unit of analysis to assess social problems such as erosion, the relations of crop performance, soils, and farming systems was a further contribution to linking culture and nature.

Hypes (1944), as noted elsewhere, equated soil erosion with human erosion and called on the agriculture experiment station to chart a research agenda on the human factor in soil erosion problems. He suggested that decline in quality of human culture and increase in social welfare might be linked to soil conditions. One impression that can be gained from the writings of the day is that maintenance of the collectivity (i.e., community) suffered when soil erosion was a problem. If soil erosion was a problem then the landowner or occupant spent much energy restoring the land. Little energy remained to contribute to sustaining the community. E. C. Weeks (1986), in discussing a natural resource system in decline, reports an analogous problem in declining forestry towns. As the natural resource on which a community depends declines, he suggests community stability declines, in large part, because those people who are most involved with the many voluntary activities to sustain community organizations and public services (the collectivity) must divert those efforts to restoring the resource or must leave the area in search of employment elsewhere.

Forestry and Agriculture

In this early period, forestry as a primary production activity received some research attention by rural sociologists particularly in the southern states. Issues of soils and the agriculture-forestry connection were addressed. Much of the early work on the sociology of forestry focused on the loss of forests to agricultural production and forest management practices that ignored reforestation. Several writers discussed the problems of forest clearing for agriculture crop production. They noted the inappropriate farming practices associated with soils, including cropping systems, which depleted soil nutrients, and attempting to raise crops in soils inappropriate to their growth (Long and Kifer, 1928). In the South, one author noted, the conversion of forestland to cotton production reduces the humus and land potential for ever returning to forestry. Crop cultivation on former forest hillsides likewise creates conditions for soil erosion to occur and further undermines potential for returning the land to forests. At best, the conversion of such lands to pasture for animal grazing was preferred. In this case, research demonstrated that natural burning of pasture would prevent reforestation of unwanted trees and control brush growth—thus maintaining the pasture for dairy production—a role for which forest soils often are best suited and a political and scientific question being reexamined today in the neo-tropics.

D. W. Skelton (1946) talks about forest-agriculture interdependence—he suggests forests are Mississippi's most important natural resource and calls for improved farm management practices to protect woodlots. S. J. Record (1910) also writes that indiscriminant forest harvesting is destroying the short-leaf pine forest below the ability of the forest to reproduce naturally. In response, people with forest-dependent occupations provided labor to plant seedlings, reestablish the forest, and voluntarily protect the remaining remnant forest stands. Their dependence on the forest was clearly recognized. However, Harold Kaufman (1939), in his master's thesis titled "Social Factors in the Reforestation of the Missouri Ozarks," deserves credit for one of the first quantitative and systematic studies of attitudes and values of natural resources within a rural population. He describes the problems of deforestation in the Ozarks and the barriers to reforestation. The barriers, according to Kaufman, reside in culture and a conflict between old forest folkways (such as woods-burning practices, timber "scrapping," and livestock grazing) and forest conservation practices. Kaufman's surveys of the attitudes of native residents in the Ozarks is one of the first quantitative studies using attitude scales on people and forest-resource issues. His 208 interviews also give rise to a discussion of resource values and social change in a resource-dependent region. His chapter on assimilation of reforestation is in part an attempt to provide guidance for those forest officials who would work with local communities utilizing the adoption and diffusion process to instill forest conservation practices as a way of life.

R. H. Westeveld and C. H. Hammer (1937) writing about the same time as Kaufman examined the problems associated with private ownership of forest and low reforestation efforts. They discuss the multiple benefits of reforestation such as protection of watershed, erosion control, and recreation. Rural sociologists of the early 1900s even flirted with 1980 resource management issues. They called attention to the multiple use of forests as shelter belts, for the protection of soils on the farm and for the protection of vital watersheds. Forests as an alternative use of denuded lands around cities could provide beauty and esthetic value (Everitt, 1921). Evergreen forests as woodlots provide fuel, and wood for fence posts. And finally, A. L. Bakke (1913) notes the effect of smoke emissions from urban industry on vegetation. Many power and heating plant chimneys have a harmful effect on trees, shrubs, and other vegetation. To a large extent, plants serve as good indicators of smoke contamination in a community.

RURAL SOCIAL ORGANIZATION

Occurring simultaneously with the very specific studies of human actions on the biophysical environment were studies by those many rural sociologists who focused on social organization as the determining factor in human-environmental relations. These "rural systems" sociologists were interested in the relationships between agricultural production, with its associated dimensions, and the human infrastructure in rural society. Description of community settlement patterns, community distribution, farming systems, and the "rural ecology" resulting from the manipulation of natural resources was the focus of attention where the goal was to document social change in human relations in rural America. These studies had little interest in describing alternative states of nature, yet resource variables appear in their paradigms. Moreover, the interaction of man and nature held the key to many of their explanations of the human condition.

We choose to define this scholarly thread of rural sociology and disciplinary centrality in terms of a human resource system (Figure 2). In this system, emphasis is placed on the interaction of population, culture, and the biophysical environment where culture and biophysical attributes together create a distinctive community organizational form that, in turn, becomes the distinctive template by which natural resources are defined and exploited.

P. A. Sorokin, et al. (1930), in a *Systematic Source Book in Rural Sociology*, provide the foundation for a human resource system. They outline the fundamental aspects of rural social organization, which include the (1) ecological, (2) morphological, (3) institutional, and (4) cultural. The authors note that these four elements, studied in variations in space and time, account for the functioning of any group including the "rural social world" (Sorokin, et al., 1930:263). The authors provide case study examples of the interaction of these four elements in determining the organization of rural life including community forms found in Western and Central Europe, the Orient, and the Americas.

Such community descriptions of population and habitation on the land were later amplified by Smith (1953), A. Bertrand (1958), L. Nelson (1955), and C. Taylor, et al. (1955) in their respective textbooks on rural sociology. Their discussions of community forms elaborate a human resource system, and the distinctiveness that arises as culture is blended with the biological system. Agriculture villages, with their citizens' residences clustered around systems of authority, dot the earth— from the feudal estates in Europe, tribal villages in Africa, and Israeli circular villages in the Middle East to the Mormon villages in Utah and Hutterite colonies in South Dakota. The

Figure 2
Definitional Components of a Human/Natural Resource System

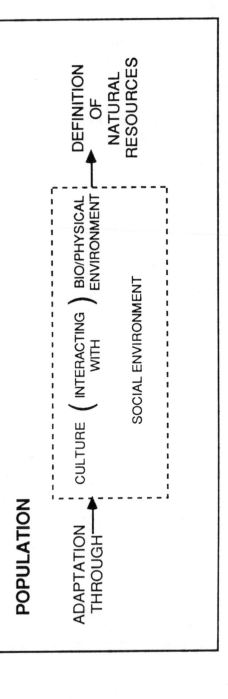

French influence on community form is documented by Smith (1953) in his description of the line village, or river front village. In this form of agricultural community, the transportation corridor defines the location of residential units on the farmstead. It is a compromise with the clustered village. Farmers occupy land, but social relations and community integration can be fostered by the proximity of one residence to another. The dispersed farmstead settlement pattern is another form of habitation of the land. Found predominately in the United States, the settlement pattern involved occupancy of the land by primary producers who were physically separated from a group or community support structure. Nevertheless, the farmer and village trade center were together defined as a community.

The New England village, the line village, and open country farm settlement pattern each represent a different organizational form to support the primary production process. The New England village, Mormon village, Hutterite village, and Israeli kibbutz represent similar forms of village settlement but with distinct cultural patterns shaping the land. The relationship of the biophysical attributes was essential in each case to understand the nature of the social organization to follow. In some cases, the biophysical environment dictated human form and personal adaptation strategies. In other cases, the biophysical environment was modified by human invention to accommodate a form of settlement. Sorokin, et al. (1930) once again provide guidance on this point. They argue that relief (topography) in regions having continuous level plains appears better adapted to groupings (villages) while mountain regions favor dispersed settlement patterns. F. Winchester (1941), who studied neighborhood and community settlement in Kentucky, is one of many who replicated these findings.

Further elaboration is provided by W. G. Mather et al. (1934) in discussing the interaction of soil structure, farm patterns and community institutional structure, in New York State; A. D. Edwards (1939) points out the consequences of drought on settlement and community stability in the West; Nelson (1952) acknowledges the relationship of religious doctrine, community structure, and farming practices in Utah; and J. V. D.

Saunders (1961) describes the organization of farming in mountainous regions of Central America, where traditional cultural patterns remain as barriers to innovations in farming practices. These are but a few examples where the interrelationship among elements of a human resource system are addressed to understand and explain human adaptation to the biophysical environment.

Many rural sociologists, however, were most intrigued by the dynamic nature of rural society and specifically by the factors associated with social change in rural organization as the natural resource system was modified by the structure of agriculture or the adoption of new farming practices that altered the farm enterprise and the balance of relations between farm and town.

A handful of writers including Zimmerman (1930), Galpin (1915), Landis (1938), and Lively (1932) devoted considerable attention to the interplay of social organization and the biophysical system. The farm-town trade center provided the sociological venue for doing so. The analysis proceeded in two interconnected ways. First, attention was directed at the association of the primary producers (farmer, forester, or miner) and the trade center that arose to serve them. These authors focused on this relationship in space and time to describe the farm towns. Like Galpin's Walworth County study, utilizing the economic institution (retail trade and farm services to delimit community boundaries), other concepts such as "Team Haul" (the distance that could be traveled by a team of horses from farm to town and return in a day) also served as a determinant of community boundaries. These students of trade center-community analysis used geographical relations to define the community-farm system. Once the system was defined, rural sociologists examined its various components. They drew attention to the changing character of the rural population—both farm and community in response to the organization of farming, including marketing practices, and specialization in the agricultural enterprise, size, and complexity of the community. Distance of farm to trade center and man-land ratio, size of farm measured in acres, were indicators of the ebb and flow of community-farm relations and the boundaries of community control.

Second, the association between and among individual community systems to form the social organization of rural America was documented. Studies by Zimmerman (1930), Lively (1932), E. Hassinger (1956), and Landis (1933) were concerned with the number, distribution, and function of rural towns across the countryside. Factors such as growth history, transportation systems, and commercialization of agriculture helped to document the evolution of rural America and how such ecological processes as competition and dominance altered human institutions on the land. In spite of the contemporary debate about the POET model and articulation of environmental variables within it (Albrecht and Murdock, 1984; Swanson and Busch 1985), a modification of O. D. Duncan's (1964) POET model illustrating the farm-trade center connection in the context of an agricultural resource region can best convey the complex ecological system some rural sociologists attempted to describe.

On the one hand, the documentation of the relationship of a constantly changing primary enterprise and its effects on a host community was essential for understanding individual community stability. The change in the size of farm, specialization within the farm enterprise, mechanization of agriculture, and marketing practices influenced farm labor requirements along with population distribution, number of farms, and changes in a specific trade center. The growth or decline of trade centers hinged on the tributary population within its geographical area of control. The POET model helps to picture the interaction of factors influencing the farm-trade center connection. On the other hand, the process of change affecting individual farm towns likewise influenced the interaction between towns and the function of such places within a given agricultural region. In other words, the factors that help to explain change between farm and town likewise help to describe the balance of relations between and among towns comprising a rural region. The dual relationship is depicted in Figure 3. Technology, in par-

Figure 3
An Ecological Model of the Interdependency Between Community and Natural Resource Region

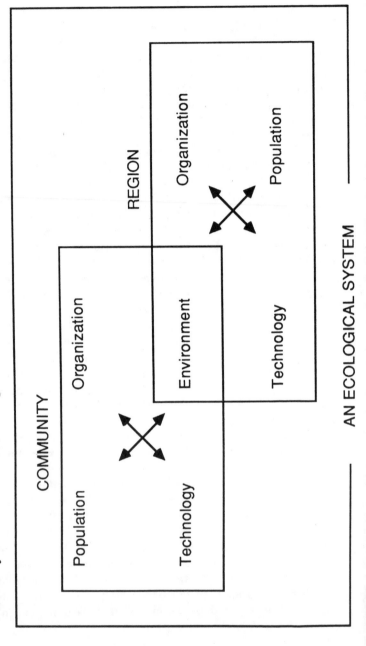

ticular, represented a perturbation to the system causing adjustment within a host community and the distribution of
communities in time and space throughout the region.

TECHNOLOGICAL CHANGE: CREATING A
NEW SOCIAL ORDER

Transportation forms and the structure of agricultural production and distribution have both operated as ecosystem factors stimulating change in the rural infrastructure (i.e.,
production process, delivery systems, distribution of towns and
farms, land tenancy, and rural institutions), in short, social
integration of rural society. Transportation systems and structure of agriculture equally (although differently) influenced
patterns of human adaptation to the rural environment. Definitions of natural resources, resulting in development of farming systems in rural society, were largely associated with these
two factors. The structure of agriculture is described in a separate volume of the fiftieth anniversary series. In this volume,
transportation is emphasized as one of the co-determinants of
an evolving rural social order where humans and resource systems together alter the distribution of numbers and kinds of
rural residents occupying the land.

Throughout the years, many articles have appeared in which
authors have discussed the factors associated with changes in
farming and trade center interdependence. One example is
Farm Trade Centers in Minnesota, 1905–1929, by Carle Zimmerman (1930). In this bulletin, the author describes the structure and function of small towns as well as the influences of
modern transportation networks on these centers. At the time
Zimmerman prepared his publication on small towns (1930),
the question of the survival of that unit in reference to larger
places was not of immediate concern. He assumed the trade
center would be an important type of community for years to
come. He was concerned, instead, with the distribution of such
places across the landscape as communities began to compete
with each other for farm business. C. R. Wasson and D. Sanderson (1933:4) describe the importance of transportation to the
restructuring of rural society. "The boundaries of a New Eng-

land town were determined by topography but it is not static. Its meaning changes with changes in the form of transportation."

Settlement in western South Dakota was encouraged by the construction of bridges across the Missouri and the subsequent rise in amount of rail connections between sections of the state. Paul Landis, writing about South Dakota in 1933, acknowledged the importance of transportation as a means of settlement and then later as a means of adjustment. Landis placed heavy emphasis on transportation as a crucial factor in the early growth and decline of trade centers.

Transportation facilities had become well established in the plains states by the 1930s. The movement of people from open country to larger trade centers and cities represents one important result of the development of transportation. The corresponding impact on the smaller trade centers is obvious. One conclusion reached by Landis concerned the future of the local trade center. The author concludes that community survival is an economic and social problem for the farmers to solve. The loss of the merchandising and marketing function and a religious or educational function would, of course, be fatal to a small community.

Landis notes a similar time perspective of drastic change in his Washington State study of small towns. The decline of the hamlet and small trade center in Washington occurred between 1900 and 1910. During this period, 210 places disappeared. An evolving transportation system released rural settlers from the constraints of nature and shifted the balance of relations among towns. The location of small towns near waterways or at the junction of two rivers greatly facilitated early trade center growth. Subsequent rail and road development had additional influences on growing and declining centers. According to the author, the relative influence of each means of travel in Washington corresponded to that found in his work in South Dakota (i.e., the growth of rail transportation, 1900–1915, and the increased use of the automobile around 1915).

Lively (1932), in his discussion, identifies 1915 as an important time when many small trade centers declined, and again according to Landis, 80 percent of growing trade centers had access to the railroad during this time. Maintaining this connection through 1930 helped stimulate growth. Only 10 percent of those trade centers that were located on a railroad declined during this period.

Lively supports the work of Zimmerman in his analysis of transportation as a force in an evolving social order in rural America. He notes the change in small towns as a reflection of business involvement with commercial agriculture, competition among centers for such business, and the availability of an adequate transportation system. The importance of the relationship between the center and a growing commercialization of agriculture in the 1930s is a decisive factor in the growth and prosperity of not only the trade center, but the farm. According to the author,

the welfare of a commercial agriculture is dependent upon the size and quality of its markets, both immediate and ultimate; also upon the nature and quality of the local trading center. The facility with which farmers may reach a trading center that can easily and efficiently receive their products and, in turn, distribute to them supplies that they demand, is closely related to their prosperity and satisfaction. (p. 3)

However, in conjunction with the development of agriculture and the growth or decline of trade centers during this period, Lively notes the continued importance of transportation. He states "the importance of transportation and communication in social organization is too well known to require elaboration here. Change in these facilities is a basic factor in the rise, decline, and realignment of groups" (p. 31).

The corresponding influence of the railroad on trade center prosperity is likewise noted. Although the presence of a railroad route provided no complete assurances of growth for the trade center, the pattern of growth favored those centers located along a railroad. Similarly the emergence of new trade centers between 1915 and 1930 was influenced by access to a railroad. In connection with advantageous location near a railroad, Lively states that "the trade center that offers ready means of transportation of farm products out of the community and of farm supplies to the community is likely to obtain and hold the support of the farm population better than its competitor that offers less along this line" (p. 34).

Changes in the farming enterprises also were noted by the author as having an influence on the trade center. A general change from grain farming to dairy farming in Minnesota caused many farmers to bypass one trade center for another with a creamery and other milk-marketing facilities. This, according to the author, stimulated growth in some of the more strategically located communities. In addition, specialization in the farm operation necessitated a complete service center to provide the range of services desired by the farmer.

ECOLOGICAL DOMINANCE IN SPACE AND TIME

Transportation systems, in particular, changed the picture of the countryside; first in terms of settlement patterns, then in successive adaptations of communities to time and space as the mode of transportation evolved. Transportation systems act as a series of constraints, opportunities, and factors between towns, primary producers, and connecting links for distribution of products to market. Whether we focus on rail, automobile, or air travel, these are networks established across the landscape to facilitate a mode of travel and transportation of goods and services. As one network gives way to another, the location and distribution of community trade centers is affected.

The construction of new and improved roads that linked towns together had a profound effect on community dominance. As transportation improved, the trade centers were able to exert an influence over a wider resource region. "Rural trade center dominance" was a concept employed to describe the spatial relations among communities. As one community became dominant, other rural communities in the immediate environs lost their function and declined. As Zimmerman (1930) notes, farmers tended to trade predominantly at one center, usually the closest, by sheer necessity. But when better roads were constructed in the rural area, farmers often traded in several centers, depending on the goods desired and the variety of goods available. The problem facing the trade center was apparent. It had to attract customers from a larger trade area. Zimmerman (1930) points out that "families that once lived in the area of one or two centers were thrown into the area of several dozens of centers. An increase in the possibilities of travel to the trade center from 4 to 15 miles increased the area of the trade community from 50 square miles to 706 square miles" (p. 37).

As one might expect, the communities to be affected first by an improved transportation system were those communities that were not located on a transportation route. These towns were usually under 500 in population and included many neighborhoods. Whereas physical and social isolation preserved these very small hamlets, a developing road and rail system reduced the need for their existence. J. H. Kolb (1933) puts the process into perspective. He described the succession in trade and visiting patterns of rural inhabitants. The decline in importance of rural neighborhoods resulted from loss of function to neighboring communities. As the community began to duplicate the services of the neighborhood, especially in terms of the school and retail establishments, the importance of those services in the neighborhood declined and established the community as a dominant unit. This occurred in many other areas formerly served by the neighborhood. The same process of competition and succession occurred between small and large rural communities. Subsequently these changes altered the marketing behavior of the farmer.

Several points can be made about the surviving trade centers. They were larger and fewer in number and their complexity increased. The concentration of services in these centers allowed the addition of further specialized services. The larger centers (primarily over 1000) prospered as centralization of function occurred. According to Zimmerman (1930), "appearing trade centers are those that have developed to meet the needs of agriculture and of local community life and those that have developed as the population bases of certain new industries and needs" (p. 32).

The growth and decline of agricultural trade centers in South Dakota parallels the trends identified by Lively (1932) and Zimmerman in Minnesota. Settlement of farmland in this section of the country took place as part of the western migration. The eastern half of the state was settled by homesteaders ahead of the western half partly because of soil and climate features. D. Chittick (1955) attributes rural settlement patterns in this area to be due in part to inadequate transportation. According to Chittick, "before the railroads, eastern South Dakota was settled almost entirely by rural farm population served by numerous hamlets and small villages. This scattered pattern of small trade centers was based largely on short distances, limited to ox or horse drawn conveyances, between towns" (p. 14).

The rise of numerous trade centers can be attributed to the nature of farming. Agricultural methods and transportation facilities at the time required numerous small trade centers to service the unprecedented number of homesteaders.

It is interesting to note the compounding nature of the various factors on trade center dominance. Competition and distance are key factors identified by Landis (1933) in trade center survival. Distance could here be defined in both a physical and a time dimension. Trade centers could be affected by competition if the travel time between centers was reduced as well as the actual physical distance between centers. Such may have been the case as transportation improved. Landis notes that prior to 1900, many trade centers were located in close proximity and a lack in the means of travel between centers insured survival. Competition was thus minimal for many items. The rise of rail transportation after 1900 increased the probability of competition from trade centers located on these routes. The period from 1900 to 1920 also witnessed the growing use of the automobile as a means of transporting products to markets and families to various trade centers for shopping purposes. Accordingly, Landis notes this same period as one of the greatest adjustments for the appearance and disappearance of trade center communities.

Improved roads and increasing use of the automobile for farm and family spelled trouble for many small centers. At the time the article was written, Landis (1933) indicates the importance of the car for trade center survival during the prior eighteen years. Without the automobile, many small trade centers could maintain the trade function for which they were established.

But with the increased use of the automobile, the communities failed to survive. According to Lively, "during this time many small trade centers have been thrown into competition with larger and more distant centers and, having no sound basis of existence except the monopoly of trade arising out of isolation, have been unable to survive the conflict and have declined or even disappeared entirely" (p. 32).

The detailed description of competition among farm towns for survival is essentially an ecological story about resource-dependent communities adjusting to changes in the primary production process. As such, the research represents a continuous record of research to support contemporary social impact assessment.

SOCIAL IMPACT ASSESSMENT (SIA) ASSOCIATED WITH RESOURCE-DEPENDENT COMMUNITIES

For the rural sociologist, the structure of agriculture, technological change, the processes of urbanization, and rural industrialization were "social impacts" affecting rural community stability, patterns of growth, or patterns of decline for a trade center in the rural area during the 1900–1950 period. Small trade centers more distant from larger trade centers and cities declined first. The importance of a rural population to a trade center is noted by Landis.

South Dakota towns are for the most part trading points for a rural population surrounding them. Take away the rural population and the greater number of them will disappear; increase the rural population and they will prosper and perhaps even increase in numbers. Tributary population is probably the greatest single factor in the success or failure in the growth of a town. (p. 30)

Thus population structure, numbers, distribution, and interdependence with a community—each becomes a crucial indicator measure for impact assessment.

Lively (1932) compares forestry, mining, and agriculture trade centers when he discusses the importance of population shifts, regional differences, and individual farm prosperity. He notes that the growth and decline of trade centers in Minnesota correspond to the economic base of a region. In areas of mining and lumbering, the growth of trade centers was slower than in areas of agriculture and high population density. In addition, the size of those places in mining areas (primarily northern Minnesota) was smaller, and a larger number of such places tended to decline during the 1930s. In sections of the state where cities and places over 2500 appeared, the growth of smaller trade centers was more certain, although the number of such places likewise declined. Hansen (1923) reports the ripple effect of the loss of forestry employment for other employment sectors and small-town tax base.

Landis' (1938b) *Three Iron Mining Towns* is perhaps the earliest comprehensive examination of the process of resource extraction, human infrastructure, and social change. Clearly a classic piece to be included in the social impact literature, Landis' work traces the discovery, establishment, and development of iron-ore production in the Mesabi Range, Minnesota, with concomitant human infrastructure development. He discusses the nature and kind of population present during different periods of ore production, evolution of a community structure, and establishment of distinctive cultural patterns. His chart (1936:131) provides a picture of human and biophysical cycles characteristic of many resource-dependent communities and regions today. One contribution of this work that should not go unnoticed is the dynamic nature of resource-dependent communities and the interacting social and biological cycles associated with such communities.

Harold and Lois Kaufman (1946) followed Landis in a detailed documentation of a forestry town in transition. Their analysis provides both a substantive contribution to the study of resource dependent-communities undergoing change and a picture of the process of conducting applied research for the U.S. Forest Service. Kaufmans' community study is a classic in the rural sociology tradition. They merit recognition for their discussion of forest economy and forest policy affecting small communities and the subsequent implications for the concept of sustained yield, the inherent instability of resource-depend-

ent communities, and the consequences of the growth and decline cycle on community institutions.

With regard to applied research, the final report including
transmittal letters is enlightening. On the one hand, the Forest
Service acknowledges receipt of the report while disassociating
itself from the conclusions. On the other, academic adminis-
trators highlight the academic quality of the report, while acknowledging the Forest Service prerogative, based on
established national policy, to disagree with the conclusions.

In general terms, the majority of the writers of the period
focused on the relationship of population and technological
change as joint perturbations altering the resource-based community and hinterland ties. In the late nineteenth and early
twentieth centuries, agricultural technology was relatively undeveloped, as compared to the 1980s. Farming was a family
operation and production was geared more toward family needs
than toward national markets. Limited technology fostered
farming as a way of life, and stimulated close ties between
farm and village. The farmer was not a specialist. He raised a
variety of products primarily for his own needs. If a surplus
occurred, then consideration was given to selling or trading for
non-farm goods available in the village. As the farmer became
a specialist and employed additional machinery, dependence
on the village lessened and economic horizons broadened.
Farming as a way of life gave way to farming as a specialized
business with corresponding loss of social and economic linkages to a given community.

Similar patterns of change have been noted in the forest
industry. Technology of the early twentieth century supported
the proliferation of family (small business) logging and milling
operations. Forest milling operations in New England were as
much a fixture in the rural community scene as the grain el-
evator was in Midwest farm-trade centers. Many such firms
prospered through the 1950s; but as timber supply declined,
preferred species declined; and as forest technology changed,
small firms declined, and with them those communities dependent on forestry. In certain ways, the resource specialist is
epitomized by the large capital-intensive forestry operations of
the West. Those operations, with its gangs of single males,

dominated the industry from northern California to Vancouver Island. But even in the West, however, forestry at the margin provided a home for the gypo logger and other family operations. Documentation of the interplay of a natural resource system undergoing transformation (commercialization, technological modernization, size of scale, etc., in resource extractive industries) and associated response by community institutional structure provide early reference points for social impact assessment (SIA). It is clear that the nature of the product and the nature of the terrain shapes social organization.

Similarly, those numerous studies focusing on the reorganization and distribution of trade centers resulting from a changing rural transportation system can be examined as studies in SIA. Most have been noted elsewhere and will not be repeated here. Nevertheless, the careful student of SIA would examine these case studies to assess contemporary resource issues and the precarious balance between the harvest of nature and a rural social order.

Industrialization as a Social Impact

The contemporary study of SIA would likewise benefit from the early work on industrialization of rural America associated with agriculture. This work documented the consequences of a change in the resource management activity itself (agriculture) and then in the ebb and flow of an urban industrial process on farms and towns.

The mechanization of agriculture has rarely been referred to as the first phase of industrialization of rural America, but it well could be. The literature on mechanization suggests it may have been the impetus for the beginning of reformation of community and institutional structure in rural America. The industrialization of agriculture continues today.

Industrialization of the farm and mechanization of agriculture offers an early glimpse of the "social impacts" on rural neighborhoods and rural communities. Studies by M. E. John (1940) and R. McMillan (1949) each describe the consequences of mechanization of agriculture on structure and operation of the farm, migration of rural youth to the city, decline in tenant farming, and related disruptions. The impact of farm mechanization on the growth and decline of the trade center community can best be described in terms of the consequences for the farm operation itself. The relationship between farm and trade center has previously been established. Therefore, we would expect that any change in the farm operation as it affects the farm population would have a corresponding effect on the community. As farmers turned more toward machinery for farm work, the additional costs required a large operation to compensate for the overall investment. Subsequently, farms became larger. For the community, this meant fewer farm families were living in a given trade area.

The capital outlay required for farm mechanization discouraged many farmers from continuing in farming, especially the operators of smaller land holdings. The number of tenant farmers decreased. In addition, the opportunities for farm youth to enter farming diminished, leading to the out-migration of many of the younger rural residents. The capital outlay for mechanization not only encouraged commercialization but helped transform the farmer from a "generalist" producing a little of everything to a "specialist" in single-species agriculture, interested in producing only a few commodities for market.

Non-agricultural industrialization of rural communities represents a change in the employment composition of a town, an employment structure heavily dominated by the service sector for most farm-trade centers. Shifts in employment often lead to alteration in numerous aspects of social structure of the community (Field, 1968). Studies of the establishment of military reservations in rural areas and construction of major dams such as Hoover Dam in Nevada, Grand Coulee Dam in Washington, Roosevelt Dam in Arizona, Oahe Dam in South Dakota, and Glen Canyon Dam in Arizona, during the 1910 to 1960 period, provide graphic pictures of changes in the sociocultural fabric of a community.

Contemporary social impact assessment studies likewise draw attention to the labor force composition as a key determinant of change and alteration of the social and cultural fabric of small communities. But industrialization as process had a dual effect on rural America, first drawing an employable labor force from the country to the city and then, during periods of rural industrialization, sending a new labor force to the country. Rural communities that were once described as "fished-out ponds" due to out-migration of their youth became, in some cases, urban satellite work centers for industrial corporations such as Hewlett-Packard. Many of the early migration studies describe the differential impact on host communities and provide verification for current assessments of resource-dependent communities undergoing change. G. K. Bowles (1957), for example, has documented the high dependent population in many small towns as a result of the loss of labor due to work shortage and consequences for community services, tax structure, etc. In many rural areas, a large proportion of the people are in the age groups comprising children under eighteen and adults over sixty-five. The majority of those that migrate are working-age adults. C. L. Beale (1964) reports in his early studies, that 60 percent of those who migrate are under twenty years old. Writers have from time to time noted differences among rural out-migrants in education, personality type, and gender. Because of fewer occupational alternatives, out-migration of farm youth was extremely heavy.

Thus population structure, including selective migration, disruption of personal bonds to a community as newer agriculture practices eliminated the dependency on a town, and industrialization of the country that brought a new labor force to a community, represents documented processes of change for contemporary SIA analysis. Like other resource-dependent communities, agricultural towns appear to have their own boom-bust cycle.

CONCLUSION

Resource-dependent communities may be unique in that the primary production processes and changes therein have direct consequences for community stability. This chapter has documented how some studies by rural sociologists examined associations between the biological regularities of a natural resource system and association for human welfare, while other studies considered how the shift from farming as a way of life to single-species agriculture had measurable consequences for community ties and integration of people into the social fabric of community affairs. Human alterations to the biophysical environment due to transportation systems and agricultural practices induced alteration to the kind and distribution of communities in rural America. Finally, resource cycles themselves are associated with the ebb and flow of community life, population, and institutional structure. This early careful documentation by rural sociologists of the interaction between the social and the biological systems provides a continuity of thought that enhances our present ability to predict human actions on the environment (Figure 4).

Specifically, the small-town research undertaken by Landis (1933), Zimmerman (1930), Chittick (1955), E. Hassinger (1956), and, later, by G. V. Fuguitt and his students at University of Wisconsin (Fuguitt and Deeley, 1966; Fuguitt and Thomas, 1966; Fuguitt and Field, 1972; Johansen and Fuguitt, 1984) is valuable in understanding social and demographic change within communities (i.e., assessment of specific factors of change for rural social organization). The influence of such factors as location and distribution of farms across the rural landscape, size of community, history of growth or decline, and location vis-à-vis metropolitan urban centers are essential predictive variables for use in future studies of patterns of change. Sociologists are indeed fortunate when longitudinal data exist to monitor and describe social change resulting from a particular action or series of events. Certainly, environmental sociologists have lamented the lack of such data bases to describe the consequences of human actions on the environment. Secondary data from the census on small towns have been systematically maintained at the University of Wisconsin, Department of Rural Sociology for the past thirty years. The data, containing population figures for small towns since 1890–1900 and social demographic characteristics of small-town residents since the mid-1960s, provide important information for those of us concerned with community-natural resource relationships in rural America. Information from forestry, wildlife,

Figure 4
Trends in Rural Sociological Studies on Human/Nature
Interaction

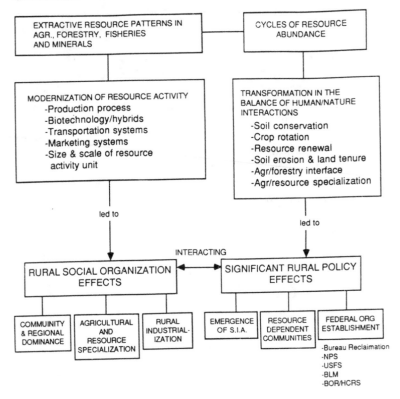

and agriculture (i.e., biological parameters such as land under tillage, board feet, stumpage value harvested, etc.) can be added as variables in our analysis of community and ecosystem change over time. Ecological processes of settlement, adaptation, and succession unfold in such a drawing. The next chapter will examine how the emergence of natural resource sociology for all of its new specifics, at times replays on themes established in earlier studies.

REFERENCES

Farming Practices and Soil Erosion

Benton, A. H. 1918. *Farm Tenancy and Leases*. St. Paul: University of Minnesota Agricultural Experiment Station Bulletin No. 178.

Brown, P. E. 1914. *The Fertility of Iowa Soils*. Ames: Iowa State College Agricultural Experiment Station Bulletin No. 150.

Buie, T. S. 1944. "The land and the rural church." *Rural Sociology* 9:251–257.

Davidson, L. A. 1943. *Soil Management Practices Recommended for Tunica County*. Mississippi State: Mississippi State University Agricultural Experiment Station Bulletin No. 381.

Gillette, J. M. 1949. "Crop response as a testing ground for geo-cultural regionalism." *Rural Sociology* 14:51–58.

Hypes, J. L. 1944. "Social implications of soil erosion." *Rural Sociology* 9:364–376.

Johnson, O. R., and W. E. Foard. 1914. *Land Tenure*. Columbia: University of Missouri Agricultural Experiment Station Bulletin No. 121.

Mordoff, R. A. 1925. *The Climate of New York State*. Ithaca, New York: Cornell University Agricultural Experiment Station Bulletin No. 444.

Schickele, R., J. P. Himmel, and R. M. Hurd. 1935. *Economic Phases of Erosion Control in Southern Iowa and Northern Missouri*. Ames: Iowa State College Agricultural Experiment Station Bulletin No. 333.

Smith, D. D., D. M. Whitt, and M. F. Miller. 1948. *Cropping Systems for Soil Conservation*. Missouri Agricultural Experiment Station Bulletin No. 518.

Smith, T. Lynn. 1953. *The Sociology of Rural Life*. New York: Harper and Brothers.

Wakely, Ray E. 1936. "Social and economic effects of soil erosion." *Rural Sociology* 1:509–510.

Weeks, Edward C. 1986. "Mill closures in the Pacific Northwest: the consequence of economic decline in rural industrial communities." In *First National Symposium on Social Science in Resource Management: Program Abstracts*, 30. Corvallis: Oregon State University 86–4, Cooperative Park Studies Unit.

Wilson, Warren H. 1912. *The Evolution of the County Community*. Boston: The Pilgrim Press.

Sociology and Forestry

Bakke, A. L. 1913. *The Effect of City Smoke on Vegetation*. Ames: Iowa State College Agricultural Experiment Station Bulletin No. 145.

Everitt, J. S. 1921. *Working Plans for a Communal Forest for the Town of Ithaca, New York*. Ithaca, New York: Cornell Uni ˌrsity Agricultural Experiment Station Bulletin No. 404.

Kaufman, Harold. 1939. "Social factors in the reforestation of the Missouri Ozarks." M.A. thesis, University of Missouri, Columbia.

Long, L. E., and R. S. Kifer. 1928. *Systems of Farming for the Hill Sections of Mississippi*. Mississippi State: Mississippi State University Agricultural Experiment Station Bulletin No. 257.

Record, S. J. 1910. *Forest Conditions of the Ozark Region of Missouri*. Columbia: University of Missouri Agricultural Experiment Station Bulletin No. 89.

Skelton, D. W. 1946. *Farm Forestry in Mississippi*. Mississippi State: Mississippi State University Agricultural Experiment Station Bulletin No. 432.

Westveld, R. H., and C. H. Hammer. 1937. *Forest Restoration in Missouri*. Columbia: University of Missouri Agricultural Experiment Station Bulletin No. 392.

Rural Social Organization and the Environment

Albrecht, Don E., and Steve H. Murdock. 1984. "Toward a human ecological perspective on part-time farming." *Rural Sociology* 49:389–411.

Bertrand, Alvin. 1951. *Agricultural Mechanization and Social Change in Rural Louisiana*. Baton Route: Louisiana State University Agricultural Experiment Station Bulletin No. 458.

Bertrand, Alvin. 1958. *Rural Sociology*. New York: McGraw-Hill.

Duncan, Otis Dudley. 1964. "Social organization and the ecosystem." In *Handbook of Modern Sociology*, ed. Robert Farris, 36–82. New York: Rand McNally.

Edwards, Allen D. 1939. "The sociology of drought." *Rural Sociology* 4:190–202.

Galpin, C. J. 1915. *The Social Anatomy of an Agricultural Community*. Madison: University of Wisconsin Agricultural Experiment Station Bulletin No. 34.

Hassinger, Edward. 1956. "Factors associated with population changes in agricultural trade center of southern Minnesota 1940–1950." Ph.D. dissertation, University of Minnesota, Minneapolis.

Landis, Paul H. 1933. *The Growth and Decline of South Dakota Trade Centers 1901–1933*. Brookings: South Dakota State University Agricultural Experiment Station Bulletin No. 279.

Landis, Paul H. 1938. *Washington Farm Trade Centers 1900–1935*. Pullman: Washington State University Agricultural Experiment Station Bulletin No. 360.

Lively, C. E. 1932. *Growth and Decline of Farm Trade Centers in Minnesota 1905–1930*. St. Paul: University of Minnesota Agricultural Experiment Station Bulletin No. 287.

Lively, C. E. 1937. "Social planning and sociology of subregions." *Rural Sociology* 8:287–298.

Mather, W. G., Jr., T. H. Townsend, and Dwight Sanderson. 1934. *A Study of Rural Community Development in Waterville, New York*. Ithaca, New York: Cornell University Agricultural Experiment Station Bulletin No. 608.

Nelson, Lowry. 1952. *The Mormon Village*. Salt Lake City: University of Utah Press.

Nelson, Lowry. 1955. *Rural Sociology*. New York: American Book Company.

Saunders, J. V. D. 1961. "Man-land relations in Ecuador." *Rural Sociology* 26:57–69.

Smith, T. Lynn. 1953. *The Sociology of Rural Life*. New York: Harper and Brothers.

Sorokin, Pitirim A., Carle C. Zimmerman, and C. J. Galpin. 1930. "Ecology of the rural habitat." In *Systematic Source Book in Rural Sociology*, Vol. 1, 263–304. St. Paul: University of Minnesota Press.

Swanson, Louis, and L. Busch. 1985. "A part-time farming model reconsidered: a comment on a POET model." *Rural Sociology* 50:427–436.

Taylor, Carl C., Arthur F. Raper, Douglas Ensminger, Margaret J. Hagood, et al. 1955. *Rural Life in the United States*. New York: A. A. Knopf.

Winchester, Frank. 1941. *Rural Neighborhoods and Communities in Thirteen Kentucky Counties, 1941: Size, Population and Social Structure*. Lexington: Kentucky Agricultural Experiment Station Bulletin No. 450.

Zimmerman, Carle C. 1930. *Farm Trade Centers in Minnesota, 1905–1929*. St. Paul: University of Minnesota Agricultural Experiment Station Bulletin No. 269.

Technology and the Production Process

Landis, Paul H. 1933. *The Growth and Decline of South Dakota Trade Centers 1901–1933*. Brookings: South Dakota State University Agricultural Experiment Station Bulletin No. 279.

Landis, Paul H. 1938a. *Washington Farm Trade Centers 1900–1935*. Pullman: Washington State University Agricultural Experiment Station Bulletin No. 360.

Lively, C. E. 1932. *Growth and Decline of Farm Trade Centers in Minnesota 1905–1930*. St. Paul: University of Minnesota Agricultural Experiment Station Bulletin No. 287.

Wasson, C. R., and Dwight Sanderson. 1933. *Relation of Community Areas to Town Government in the State of New York*. Ithaca, New York: Cornell University Agricultural Experiment Station Bulletin No. 555.

Zimmerman, Carle C. 1930. *Farm Trade Centers in Minnesota, 1905–1929*. St. Paul: University of Minnesota Agricultural Experiment Station Bulletin No. 269.

Ecological Dominance

Kolb, J. H. 1933. *Trends of County Neighborhoods: 1921–1931*. Madison: University of Wisconsin Agricultural Experiment Station Bulletin No. 120.

Landis, Paul H. 1933. *The Growth and Decline of South Dakota Trade Centers 1901–1933*. Brookings: South Dakota State University Agricultural Experiment Station Bulletin No. 279.

Lively, C. E. 1932. *Growth and Decline of Farm Trade Centers in Minnesota 1905–1930*. St. Paul: University of Minnesota Agricultural Experiment Station Bulletin No. 287.

Zimmerman, Carle C. 1930. *Farm Trade Centers in Minnesota, 1905–1929*. St. Paul: University of Minnesota Agricultural Experiment Station Bulletin No. 269.

Social Impact Assessment

Beale, C. L. 1964. "Rural depopulation in the United States." *Demography* 1:264–272.

Bowles, Gladys K. 1957. "Migration patterns." *Rural Sociology* 22:1–11.

Field, Donald R. 1968a. "The impact of employment alternatives on a growing rural community." Ph.D. thesis, The Pennsylvania State University.

Hansen, T. S. 1923. *Second Growth on Cut-Over Lands in St. Louis County*. St. Paul: University of Minnesota Agricultural Experiment Station Bulletin No. 203.

John, M. E. 1940. *Forces Influencing Rural Life*. University Park: Pennsylvania State Agricultural Experiment Station Bulletin No. 308.

Kaufman, Harold F., and Lois C. Kaufman. 1946. "Toward the stabilization and enrichment of a forest community: *The Montana Study*." Missoula: University of Montana.

Landis, Paul H. 1933. *The Growth and Decline of South Dakota Trade Centers 1901–1933*. Brookings: South Dakota State University Agricultural Experiment Station Bulletin No. 279.

Landis, Paul H. 1938a. *Washington Farm Trade Centers 1900–1935*. Pullman: Washington State University Agricultural Experiment Station Bulletin No. 360.

Landis, Paul H. 1938b. *Three Iron Mining Towns: A Study in Cultural Change*. Ann Arbor, Michigan: Edwards Brothers.

Lively, C. E. 1932. *Growth and Decline of Farm Trade Centers in Minnesota 1905–1930*. St. Paul: University of Minnesota Agricultural Experiment Station Bulletin No. 287.

McMillan, Robert. 1949. *Social Aspects of Farm Mechanization in Oklahoma*. Stillwater: Oklahoma Agricultural Experiment Station Bulletin No. 339.

Zimmerman, Carle C. 1930. *Farm Trade Centers in Minnesota, 1905–1929*. St. Paul: University of Minnesota Agricultural Experiment Station Bulletin No. 269.

Conclusion

Chittick, Douglas. 1955. *Growth and Decline of South Dakota Trade Centers 1901–1951*. Brookings: South Dakota State University Agricultural Experiment Station Bulletin No. 448.

Fuguitt, Glen V., and Nora Ann Deeley. 1966. "Retail service patterns and small town population change: a replication of Hassinger's study." *Rural Sociology* 31:53–63.

Fuguitt, Glen V., and Donald R. Field. 1972. "Some population characteristics of villages differentiated by size, location and growth." *Demography* 9:295–308.

Fuguitt, Glen V., and D. W. Thomas. 1966. "Small town growth in

the United States: an analysis by size, class and by place."
Demography 3:513–527.

Hassinger, Edward. 1956. "Factors associated with population changes in agricultural trade center of southern Minnesota 1940–1950." Ph.D. dissertation, University of Minnesota, Minneapolis.

Johansen, H. E., and G. V. Fuguitt. 1984. *The Changing Rural Village in America*. Cambridge, Massachusetts: Ballinger Publishing Co.

Landis, Paul H. 1933. *The Growth and Decline of South Dakota Trade Centers 1901–1933*. Brookings: South Dakota State University Agricultural Experiment Station Bulletin No. 279.

Zimmerman, Carle C. 1930. *Farm Trade Centers in Minnesota, 1905–1929*. St. Paul: University of Minnesota Agricultural Experiment Station Bulletin No. 269.

2

Expanding the Domain of Nature

The founding of the Rural Sociological Society was based on the assumption that rural communities, farm families, and their way of life would continue to be a central and distinctive aspect of American society. Though the United States became more urban than rural by the end of the 1920s, the primary production states of the South, Midwest and the West remained comfortably agricultural and rural. For these areas, rural electrification, soil conservation practices, new seeds, better irrigation systems, fertilizers and herbicides, better roads, and some government protection of grazing rights and crop prices were the really important environmental issues through the Second World War. In general, the U.S. Department of Agriculture (USDA), its extension services, and similar government agencies dedicated to increasing farm productivity and life quality in rural areas were the major alternatives to academic employment for rural sociologists.

THE DECLINE OF AGRICULTURAL COMMUNITIES

By the late 1950s, the facts were running against this view of rural America. There was a steady loss of farms, farmers, and farm-trade centers. As table 1 illustrates, only twenty states had over half of their population in rural areas in 1950.

By 1960, the number of rural states was reduced to twelve, in 1970 it was nine, and in 1980 it was seven. These changes reflect increasing concentration of farm ownership and the industrial organization of agriculture. All of these trends meant an ever declining supply of subjects for traditional rural sociological research. Meanwhile, the high tech, high capital intensive agriculture combined with new forms of electronic communication and improved transportation systems further blurred distinctions between the country and the city. Therefore, by all the usual portents, it seemed as if rural sociology would be an endangered academic specialty sometime in the 1960s.

The story of rural America was clear as Lyle Schertz (1979) argues.

Farm numbers will continue to decline, the number of larger farms will increase, and, in turn, the average size of farms (measured by acres or by sales) will increase. An indication of the possible changes in the mix of different sizes of farms is provided by [Figure 5]. [This figure] depict[s] the historical numbers of farm sizes as measured by acres and by sales. The values portrayed for the year 2000 in [this figure] are trend values reported by Lin.

These estimates suggest that if past trends continue, the farms at the end of the century with 500 acres or more and farms with sales of greater than $40,000 will increase in number. The biggest decreases will occur among the smaller farms. Projections included in two other research reports also suggest that farms will number between 1 to 2 million in 2000. (p. 41)

Another indicator of changes in farm size is that of estimates of the number of farmers that account for selected percentages of total farm sales and land in farms (Figure 5).

A factor encouraging the trend toward bigness has been a steady decline in the farm labor force and a significant increase in capital inputs. As the Schertz (1979) study reports,

in 1950, labor accounted for almost 40 percent of the value of all resources used in farming; by 1977, it had declined to 14 percent. In 1950, capital (machinery and chemicals) accounted for 25 percent of all resources used in farming; by 1977, it had increased to 43 percent.

Figure 5
Number of Farms by Size, Class, and Sales

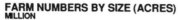

FARM NUMBERS BY SIZE (ACRES)
MILLION

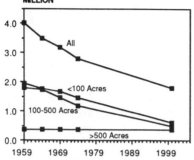

All

<100 Acres

100-500 Acres

>500 Acres

1959 1969 1979 1989 1999

NUMBER OF FARMS BY SIZE (SALES CLASS)
MILLION

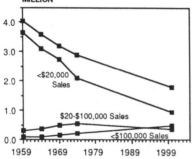

<$20,000 Sales

$20-$100,000 Sales

<$100,000 Sales

1959 1969 1979 1989 1999

NUMBER OF LARGEST FARMS
WITH 50 PERCENT OF TOTAL SALES
AND LAND IN FARMS
THOUSAND

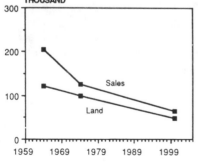

Sales

Land

1959 1969 1979 1989 1999

Source: Schertz, Lyle P. and others
(1979) Another Revolution in U.S.
Farming? Economics Statistics and
cooperative Service, Agr. Economic
Report, 441   P. 77 and 78
USDA, Washington, D.C.

The shift in resource mix, showing a substantial substitution of capital goods for labor, reflects the changing productivity of inputs and changes in the relative prices of these inputs. (p. 32)

It is clear that the rancher and the farmer are squeezed in peculiar ways by our political economy. The large-scale corporations are found in only a few specialty areas—feedlots, large-scale vegetable and fruit growing, and processing operations. The high capital and land costs, the unpredictable variations of weather and nature and the returns of 3 to 4 percent on investment are seldom attractive to large corporations. They dominate at both ends of production—they supply the equipment, fertilizers and so forth, and they control the processing and distribution of agricultural products. The family farmer is at the mercy of oligopolies that can manage prices, while he must endure all the up and down whims of the free market.

Further, the decades from 1930 to 1970 accelerated the substitution of high energy technology for labor. Yet the gains from high energy technology and fertilizers seem to be peaking at about the same time that their high costs are making them less desirable components of farm production. Studies by D. Pimentel, et al. (1973), J. S. Steinhart and C. E. Steinhart (1974), E. Hirst (1974), L. Brown (1975), and others, all demonstrate that the U.S. food system—from farm to home—since the 1940s has spent more energy than it has gained from food production. The present subsidy is around ten calories for every calorie gained. It is obvious that such deficit spending will not continue for many decades—especially not in a world that anticipates seven billion people within twenty-five years and a declining pool of expendable energy.

Plant geneticists are generally bullish on the prospects for ever expanding agricultural production, yet Professor Neal Jensen (1978:317) has argued that

the dramatic increases in wheat yields that began in the mid-1930s in the United States will soon begin to level off. The favorable mix of genetics and technology that has characterized this era must build upon an ever higher yield base for the future. At the same time the residue of factors that can lower wheat yields includes a larger proportion of forces not easily shaped or controlled by man. An example is weather. The result is a natural yield ceiling that is already visible and that will impose a limit on future productivity growth.

It would seem that agriculture, like the managing and helping professions, deals with living systems which are ultimately subject to natural patterns beyond technological modification and control. And that of course was a message being propounded by a group of maverick and hybrid rural sociologists as early as the 1950s. They were willing to question existing sociological assumptions about man and nature. In this sense, these scientists began to elevate the importance of nature as a biological variable within sociological models of natural resource systems.

This chapter will examine the trend from farms and farm communities to rural regions and environmental issues. It will do this in the following manner. First, natural resource sociologists by virtue of their specialized study of nature, expanded the domain of nature. Specialization was characteristic of much of the sociological enterprise during the 1950s. While ecosystem analysis lost favor, specialization did allow social scientists to explore diverse ways to define nature and incorporate measures within sociological inquiry. Often nature was viewed as a limiting factor in social outcomes. Thus the influence of nature expanded and along with it, its domain in balancing the relations between the social and the biological. Second, an emerging synthesis of the theoretical and methodological development associated with the study of natural resources in a variety of natural realms is considered. Finally, the contribution of such methodological and applied work has produced a learning curve of knowledge about the environment that follows four pathways of thought and influence—wildlands, social movements, theory, and urban-industrial patterns. Throughout this discussion, we shall assume, and often underline, the important role of the Natural Resources Research Group (NRRG) in supporting the study of the environment from the 1950s to the present.

EXPANSION THROUGH SPECIALIZATION

Members of the NRRG were looking at non-urban areas and finding that though farms, farmers, and farming were changing, there were whole new realms of rural social institutions, social behavior, and social problems awaiting the application of traditional theories and methods. The postwar boom in outdoor recreation had compelled a variety of federal and state resource agencies to discover their need for sociological imagination and data. Rural sociologists were studying family campers where once they had studied family farmers, they were systematically examining the relationship between forest management practices and community stability, they were examining the sociological aspects of human-caused forest fires, and they were advising on ways to encourage farmers in developing countries to adopt new agricultural techniques.

The 1960s established a legalistic basis that would further encourage agencies such as U.S. Army Corps of Engineers, U.S. Forest Service, Bureau of Land Management, National Park Service, and the Soil Conservation Service to contract for the services of rural sociologists. There emerged a series of federal laws and actions such as the Multiple Use Act of 1960, the Outdoor Recreation Resources Review Commission in 1962, The Wilderness Act of 1964, The National Environmental Protection Act of 1969, and the Clean Air and Water Acts in the 1970s that compelled attention to understanding rural communities.

Further, there were the dramatic changes in the American political environment. The civil rights, anti-Vietnam War, and environmental movements were major challenges to the predominant postwar concerns with stability, conformity, and middle-class materialism. Dramatic and continuous change was seen as a desired normative standard. Consequently, there were major challenges to the predominant postwar theoretical framework of sociology—structural-functionalism. Suddenly, the research based on the works of T. Parsons (1951), C. P. Loomis (1960), R. K. Merton (1968), and their intellectual children was seen as failing to deal with the central problems challenging western society. All at once, the theoretical agendas were open as well as the opportunity to challenge traditional practices of ever increasing uses of technology, capital, and energy to produce more and more agricultural surpluses.

A significant effect of these changes was the theoretical debate introduced by W. Catton and R. Dunlap (1978) and challenged by F. Buttel (1978) and others as to whether there was need to shift from a homocentric theory to a biocentric theory. Though the debate was couched in terms of "human exceptionalism" versus a "new environmental paradigm" it was another recycling of arguments about the nature and extent of biological influences and constraints on human desires and behavior. Yet, the debate was more than nature versus nurture, all over again. Some theorists were going beyond simply using biological analogies and were using the basic biological propensities of people as an operating guide for a new kind of human ecology theory. They were not just pointing in alarm to environmental crises, but were asking, "what aspects of the physical and biological environment are important determinants of human social systems and human social processes" (Richerson and McEvoy, 1976:xi). They were not denying the internal and ideal aspects of human behavior, but were raising to equal importance the external and material aspects affecting observed behavioral regularities (Campbell and Wade, 1972). They were converting to sociological variables the traditional biological ecology concerns with matter, energy, and information (Dunlap and Catton, 1979). Through such inquiry and debate the rural sociologists' domain of nature expanded.

Several other factors appeared in the changed political environment of rural sociology and they had an influence on the development of natural resources (environmental) sociology. The environmental movement politicized some biological ecologists who promptly rediscovered old sociological notions such as Spencer's social Darwinism and Malthus' dismal notions of population outrunning food supply. While the political ecologists were talking about lifeboat ethics (Hardin, 1974), limits to growth (Meadows, et al., 1974), and sociological triage (Paddock and Paddock, 1967) they were stimulating rural sociologists both to defend their turf and to correct the errors of the biologists, while at the same time, redefining and rethinking some of the older sociological theories of social behavior and rural development. Studies in ethology, sociobiology, and animal sociology were providing means for improvements in methods of observation and creating opportunities for gains in scientific rigor through cross-species comparisons. Finally, the oil supply crises of 1973–1974 reinforced the importance of biophysical constraints on certain traditional attitudes toward agricultural productivity. The supply crisis also opened a new set of resource issues for the applied research of rural sociologists.

These general changes—changes in the rural setting, changes in experiences of rural sociologists, changes in opportunities through research funds and jobs in new federal agencies, and changes in the political environment—led to the establishment of a specialist group within the society. In 1964, the rural sociologists working in the now broadened domain of nature had an official group (Sociology of Forestry Group) with Wade Andrews as its first chair. This group served as the seedbed for a similar specialty group that later emerged in the Society for the Study of Social Problems and then much later as an Environmental Sociology Section in the American Sociological Association. Indeed, many of the officers of the rural sociology group later became the founders and officers of these other groups in the other sociological societies. Furthermore, the new research group served as a home for scholars from other scientific backgrounds, such as forestry, wildlife, engineering, architecture, planning, psychology, animal studies, biology, and so forth, who were interested in the influences of environment on human behavior.

So from a situation where it seemed that the domain of rural sociology was shrinking it began to expand through specialization in a variety of natural resource issues and through biological system variables being redefined and incorporated within sociological analysis. There were new resource issues to which traditional approaches could be applied—wilderness, recreation, water management, soil conservation, forestry, park management, energy, wildlife, and so forth. There were new paradigms to consider. There were new persons from a wide range of disciplines and approaches, including some hybrids from mainline sociology. There were new methods, such as those provided by the animal behaviorists. The domain of nature that held the interests of rural sociologists was greatly expanded; furthermore, the influence of rural sociologists grew

Figure 6
Processes and Practices in Response to the Changing Environment for Natural Resource Rural Sociologists

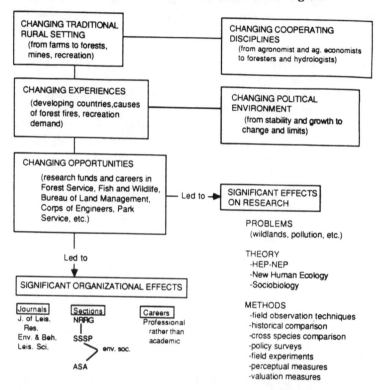

enormously within the parent discipline, within new government agencies, and in major policy decision areas.

Figure 6 outlines how a range of events converged to compel new specializations for rural sociologists at the same time that it greatly expanded the domain of research problems and explanatory variables of the discipline. The shift from studying farm systems to forest management systems and water management systems encouraged foresters, hydrologists, engineers, and others to participate at rural meetings. The wilderness and environmental movements encouraged sociologists interested in planning and urban environments to look for a supportive intellectual home and they found it in the tolerant and open organizational environment of the RSS. Rural sociologists began working in such "foreign" territories as developing countries and national forests and they found that some traditional ideas traveled well but that there also was a need for new theories and methods. And these events combined with new career opportunities in the National Park Service, Forest Service, Army Corps of Engineers, and others.

As the figure indicates, these events had significant organizational and research effects on rural sociology. Organizationally, there were new publication outlets both through the creation of additional journals and a greater tolerance by the traditional journals for natural resource topics. As noted above, in 1964, a group that subsequently would be called the Natural Resources Research Group, was formed within the Rural Sociological Society and became the seedbed for the later establishment of environmental sociology sections in the Society for the Study of Social Problems and the American Sociological Association. In the early 1960s, fulltime career positions for sociologists were established in the Forest Service with the other resource agencies not far behind.

THE INFLUENCE OF THE CHANGED ENVIRONMENT ON PROBLEMS AND TECHNIQUES

The effects on research were even more significant. There was a very large array of new problems running all the way from the patterns of outdoor recreation behavior to the social causes and consequences of noise, air, and water pollution. We have already mentioned the ferment in reconstructing human ecology theory far beyond the simplistic metaphors of the Chicago School. People were viewed as part of the ecosystem acting and being acted upon in similar manner to other organisms. The NRRG and its predecessors served as a venue for reporting findings as well as for developing new concepts and measurement techniques.

The forest recreation setting posed new problems of sampling and estimating numbers of people. There were no addresses.

The population was often widely dispersed and arrived and departed from the system at all times of the day and night. This stimulated the development of more systematic forms of observation. W. R. Burch (1964), for example, developed an observation schedule that sorted by age, gender, and activity. Burch (1965) also reported how the family camping complex exhibited a far wider range of activities than had been imagined and that there were systematic regularities of recreation behavior associated with age and gender. L. D. Love (1964) used systematic observation to estimate campsite preference and characteristic user groups. R. Lee (1975) used observation in combination with interviews to estimate factors affecting social carrying capacity. He also used trace measures such as number and distribution of camp-fire rings to estimate patterns in visitor preferences. Often, the problem was simply knowing how many people were in dispersed recreation areas such as a wilderness, and here various electronic devices were tested and calibrated with observations and/or interviews to estimate use (James and Schreuder, 1972). Consequently, the practical demands of the wildland management agencies such as the Forest Service were providing some improved measurement tools and were providing new settings for testing them.

Another traditional method given new development and testing was the use of historical comparison. The ecosystem concept forced sociologists to think in system terms rather than individualistic terms. A pioneering work was F. Cottrell's (1955) examination of the social factors that permitted the evolution of high-energy industrial systems and why there were limits to such systems and their applicability to the agrarian societies in the developing world. The petroleum shortages of the 1970s gave solid empirical proof to the ideas that Cottrell developed from sociological theory and historical data (Rosa and Machlis, 1985). Duncan's (1964) influential essay provided even longer time comparisons in his consideration of the evolution of human society from Pleistocene hunter-gatherers to modern urban-industrial societies. As he notes (1964:50), "ecological expansion, then, is carried forward by an accumulation of culture content—advances in control of the flows of materials, energy, and information—both within and between civilizations." Burch (1971) gave primary attention to the evolution of ideas about man and nature within the United States and to comparing these to other societies at different points in their history. From 1960 to 1980, A. Schnaiberg continued such historical comparison by considering distributional differences between communal (socialist) and individualistic (capitalist) patterns of social organizations and their varying impacts on the ecosystem.

The NRRG and the RSS also provided a venue for sociological consideration of cross-species comparisons. At the annual meetings in the early 1970s there were sessions that included prominent ethologists discussing the social organization of wolves, baboons, water buffalo, and dairy cows along with the usual studies of human organization. N. H. Cheek (1972) and Cheek and Burch (1976) explored the ways in which certain universals such as age and gender compelled certain patterns of social organization in humans and non-humans, at the same time they illustrated how culture built on and made unique these universal patterns. They drew on a variety of ethologists who were doing basic comparisons between species (i.e., Crook, 1970; Dolhinow, 1971; Tiger, 1969) to identify and measure what patterns people shared with all forms of social species and how they differed. The idea was that once these similarities and differences were ordered, then clearer management directives could be made for wildlands and other areas because we could determine what was mutable and what was immutable in certain human behavioral patterns. Burch (1976) followed these basic biological factors to examine empirically the role that certain unequal distributional patterns of environmental stress might play in sustaining observed class structures.

Environmental issues also encouraged rural sociologists to combine their traditional interest in rural areas with their traditional interest in application. The public policy survey was pioneered by Don Dillman (1971) who tracked the changing public values for certain problems and solutions and directed his findings to policymakers and the public at large. R. J. Burdge (1982) improved the format and considered a wide range of life quality issues in both Kentucky and Illinois. The virtue of these approaches is that there was immediate feedback to decision makers and the general public on environmental matters that usually were given little or only cursory treatment by the regular public opinion polls. The application of social science to natural resource topics has continued through the years with the support of the National Park Service, Forest Service, Bureau of Land Management, Soil Conservation Service, and Bureau of Reclamation. Government social scientists representing these agencies have reported on the application of different theoretical and methodological models in the government workplace and discussed applied science (i.e., the conduct of science in a non-scientific setting, its requirements and limitations, and the importance of science-clientele relations) (Wenner, 1985). Generally these agency scientists have expanded the research horizons of academic rural scientists to a new set of rural problems, the politics of science and resource management, and the power of effectively conducted social science in resource decision making.

Research affiliated with NRRG also developed new approaches to field experiments. T. Heberlein (1971) used a variety of ingenious ways to create a range of sanctions, to measure their relative impact on littering behavior, and to measure the factors affecting discrepancies between stated and behavioral norms. His rigorous, pioneering work led to a variety of replications (Clark, et al., 1972) and variations for other environmental issues such as the role of direct cost feedback and other incentives on patterns of energy consumption (Heberlein, 1975). The value of such research is that it permitted a more rigorous testing of basic theoretical notions about the nature, formation, and maintenance of social norms. And these are issues of central importance to both the earliest and the most recent study of rural life.

Finally, there have been substantial contributions to measuring sociological factors affecting variations in perception and valuation (willingness to pay) or level of satisfaction. All of these measurement developments have sought ways to quantify non-market values of experiential quality. R. Schreyer and J. W. Roggenbuck (1981) as H. R. Capener (1973) and others examine how varying groups respond to a similar setting. The research captures the fact that perception is not a purely physical response but is highly filtered by the nature of one's group experiences. Other studies (Lee, 1976; Bultena and Hendee, 1972) look at contrasting perceptions of potentially conflicting groups and how such variations affect behavior, policy decisions and willingness to adapt. Other studies have developed a metrics of satisfaction that approaches the finer gradations of the economists' price and costs measures (Peterson, 1974; Ditton, et al., 1982). In the newer work, survey techniques and field experiments make use of monetary measures to gain insight on the relative values that various groups have for qualitatively different experiences (Heberlein, et al., 1982; Kellert, 1982).

Though these methods add variety, rigor, and wider scope to theoretical and applied rural sociological studies, they are best used with the same caution that Heberlein (1974) offered regarding environmental problems, and scientists should avoid too easy an acceptance of any single solution. Heberlein considered the several ways we have attempted to avoid the human and material losses from floods—flood control structures, educating people to not live on floodplains, and zoning against floodplain development. His reminder that complex problems usually require more than a single solution is one worthy of application to the many current attempts at single measures of value—from dollars, to satisfaction level, to personal benefit, to social carrying capacity. Hence, the value of the NRRG as a place to try out new methods is balanced as a venue for giving humility to those that are overcertain of their universal application.

CONTINUITY OF IDEAS AND APPROACHES—
FOUR PATHWAYS OF INFLUENCE

With this outline as a map to events and their impact on natural resources sociology in particular and rural sociology theory and methods in general, we can do some more detailed exploration of particular paths of influence on social scientific ideas and practices. Influence is treated as a two-way thoroughfare, such that producers and recipients of ideas exist symbiotically. Students of urban environmental effects are influenced by the models and methods of rural sociologists as, in turn, the corpus of rural sociology is broadened by using models, findings, and methods of the urban environmental sociologists. Four broad problem loci of influence pathways are identified—wildlands, social movements, environmentalism, and urban-industrial. These problem areas were and are significant arenas of thought, theories, methods of research, and applications of research that attract groups of scholars and practitioners.

Perhaps the most crucial and natural focus for rural sociology has been the groups of studies and persons interested in wildlands. Wildlands issues cover those places that are primarily non-urban and non-agricultural, though they have parts of both. Such areas include a variety of resource-dependent communities and systems—forestry, rangelands, water production, and distribution systems, mining, fishing, and nature-based tourism communities.

Wildland Influences

The bulk of ideas and findings in natural resources sociology comes from studies of recreation behavior associated with wildlands. Wildland studies are grouped into four problem areas—natural resources development influences on community change and stability, social deviation in wildland settings, institutional patterns in wildland settings, and small group behavior in wildland recreation settings. In the following pages the central tendencies of these four areas are briefly indicated.

The studies of how various management actions impact on resource-dependent communities are not unlike traditional rural sociology studies of farm communities. The primary attention is on sustainable uses that ensure continuity of a particular social form and the factors that diminish resource supply or demand, and therefore alter a community's political economy. These studies consider how certain forest practices affected employment and economic stability of dependent communities, and how Forest Service policy impacted Amerindian and other rural minorities, and they describe the social patterns associated with the rise and fall of mineral extractive boomtowns.

As Lee (1985:10) notes,

rural sociologists have long taken an interest in agricultural policy and have examined alternative institutional arrangements for improving the relationships between agricultural communities and agricultural industries (Goldschmidt 1978). Development of a corresponding interest in forest policy is only now emerging. The question of community stability and its relationship to policies governing both wood harvest rates and industrial structure is an important concern for rural sociologists.

Lee's study is one more set of data in the stream of a continuing rural sociological tradition. Early studies of the effect of a deforested region on a local community were done by Harold Kaufman (1939) where he treated the forest economy as part of the total culture. Later, Kaufman (1961) suggested guidelines for combining forestry programs with programs of community development. Kaufman's colleagues in Mississippi were equally interested in such matters. A. W. Baird (1965) described the attitudes and characteristics of forest residents whereas Wilkinson and his colleagues (e.g., Wilkinson and Hughes, 1966) were doing similar work on water resource development. The water resources area was a fertile one for considering a full range of sociological factors. An outstanding example of the breadth of such work was W. H. Andrews and D. C. Geersten (1970). They considered attitudes toward conversation and water use, the impact of social change, the diffusion of information about use, the kinds of social institutions that developed around water rights, and distribution of uses and perceptions of those uses.

Many of the early studies of resource influences on community stability and change anticipated the present interest in factors such as the influence of the scale and diversity of economic patterns on social balance. F. Barth (1959) saw culture growing out of ecology, but in turn sustaining itself through a diversity of activities. Others saw an evolution of socioeconomic patterns (Gibson, 1944), and still others saw the

matter of resources as being simply the surrogate for the
oppression of one cultural pattern by another (Knowlton, 1972).
And the concern about how "newcomers" impact on "oldtimers"
(Graber, 1974) is a lineal antecedent of the post-energy crises
boomtown studies that proliferated in the late 1970s and early
1980s (Freudenburg, 1984).

Studies on deviation in wildland settings have given most
attention to human-caused forest fires and littering and van-
dalism in forest recreation settings. Studies of fire setting have
looked at community tolerance of woods fires (Heffernan and
Welch, 1972; Fahenstock, 1964), age and gender factors associated with incendiarism (Folkman, 1972; Jones, et al., 1965;
Baird, 1969), and the design of forest fire prevention messages
(Doolittle, 1972). R. N. Clark, et al. (1972) have undertaken a
variety of studies on depreciative behaviors that find certain
age, gender, ethnic, and environmental factors influence the
observed rates of deviation. They report that the highest proportion of deviant acts are produced by only a small proportion
of the population. Heberlein (1971) used unique observational
techniques to identify group influence and incentives that affect patterns of littering. Of importance in these studies is their
consistent finding of the crucial role that normative structures
play in determining conservation behavior. This is clearest in
W. D. Heffernan and G. D. Welch's (1972:186) study where they
say, "in designing programs to encourage the conservation of
natural resources in this area, one must be concerned not with
changing the laws or the attitudes of the majority, but rather
one must attempt to change the attitudes of a small number
of somewhat isolated individuals."

Studies on institutional patterns in wildland settings cover
a wide range of institutions. There is a large body of studies
on how development projects alter family, governmental, and
other regular community solutions to recurring problems; for
example, the Andrews and Geersten (1970) study notes reciprocal influences, with institutions both constraining and responding to developments. R. N. Singh and K. P. Wilkinson
(1974) concentrate on measuring the patterns, while a study
by J. D. Photiadis (1960) is similar to a large number of studies
that measure attitudes toward development. S. Johnson and

Burdge (1974) go beyond the measurement of attitudes toward resource development projects to measure premigration stress on people who will be relocated and the stress after relocation. They, like rural sociologists who study other areas, have a strong empathy for the subjects of their study. As they note, "much sociological research has made it easier for planners" (Johnson and Burdge, 1974:185). They intend to "resist the tide of optimism that pervades much of our functionally specific research in water resources that serves to grease the wheels of bureaucracies who foster massive social change, oblivious to the real human and social costs" (Johnson and Burdge, 1974:185).

The concern with the distribution of costs and benefits attributable to natural resource activities has been a major one for rural sociologists. Papers in a workshop on social aspects of water projects (Institute for Social Science Research on Natural Resources, 1968) gave almost as much attention to equity factors as to attitudes and institutional aspects. I. A. Spaulding (1972) found significant social class differences in patterns of water consumption. Field and Cheek (1974) found class and group variations in recreational uses of water whereas Schnaiberg (1975) and C. R. Humphrey and Buttel (1982) concentrate on unequal distribution in costs and benefits of resource projects and pollution exposure. This body of studies is well within the tradition of rural sociologists who have considered agricultural systems only (e.g., Goldschmidt, 1978). One group is attempting to get farmers (or residents of natural resource regions) to accept some innovation that decision makers think will "improve" conditions and another group of rural sociologists is pointing out the high human costs and the differential impact of benefits and costs of such projects and innovations. Like rural sociologists who study only agricultural systems, natural resource sociologists are often of two minds, some are helping to encourage resource development and others are seeking to discourage or to greatly alter the nature of the development. In our applied research we wish to see improvements, and at the same time we wish to conserve ways of life threatened by the improvements.

A group of studies related to distribution of costs and benefits examines the distribution of property rights and the institutions that sustain certain differentials in that distribution. An outstanding study along that line is P. C. West's (1982) use of Weberian theory to look at the impact of Forest Service range policy on large-scale and small-scale stock ranchers in the western United States. J. D. Tarver (1963) has a more traditional spatial examination, while L. Fortmann (1985a) examines in detail the relationship between property institutions and deforestation.

Ashby (1985) provides a useful empirical study of the connection between property institutions, markets, and ecosystem decline. She (1985) found in her study of villages in Columbia that

small farms located on steep-sloped land highly susceptible to soil erosion adapt to environmental processes of soil fertility decline with cultural practices that provide them with income in the short-run but which exacerbate the long-run process of soil erosion. In this case, small farmers have responded to a market structure and a political and institutional environment, which creates incentives for them to expand cassava production. (p. 394)

In short, the institutional structures of property rights, market forces, and the household division of labor override technical "solutions" to soil erosion. Only by modifying these institutional structures in conjunction with appropriate technical factors can the peasant break the cycle of soil depletion leading to social depletion and further soil depletion.

Emerging from rural development planning in the third world are policy and theoretically relevant studies on the influence of institutionalized gender roles on natural resources practices. For the most part, this interest is a result of rising feminist consciousness in Western countries, but its significance for issues of deforestation and afforestation is crucial. Until there was an awareness of women's roles in resource practices, many conservation project failures went unexplained. Important work has been done by M. W. Hoskins (1979), P. Williams (1983), and Fortmann and D. Rocheleau (1985). However, these studies only give a hint of the large amount of literature on gender roles, most of which are in fugitive documents such as Agency for International Development (AID) and Food and Agricultural Organization (FAO) reports. Of interest is the similarity of developing country findings on division of labor and those of a study done on New York State farm households (Buttel and Gillespie, 1984). Here, these students find, as do all the other studies on gender roles, in North America and abroad, that women's economic contributions to farmstead activities are consistently underestimated.

The fourth cluster of wildland studies—small group behavior in recreation settings—has probably produced the largest literature and has been the major source of funding and employment for natural resources sociologists. These studies in particular have made four major contributions to our understanding of social behavior. First, they have generated a solid understanding of the important role that wildland settings in particular, and all recreation locales in general, provide in maintaining continuity between generations of kin. Second, they have produced solid and frequently replicated data on the sociological determinants of crowding perception and in-group–out-group effects on carrying capacity of public places. Third, they have reinforced understanding of socialization processes and emphasized the importance of wildland settings for establishing and sustaining social bonds within intimate social groups of friends and family. Fourth, they have clearly established that the primary behaving unit in wildland settings is a small social group of kin and/or other intimates.

Studies on wildland recreation are so extensive that one could write a substantial book on them alone. Even Robert Manning's (1986) excellent summary covers only a small portion of the literature. Therefore, it seems prudent to remind readers that there could be many more contributions identified from the literature. However, it seems that the four major contributions we have identified—value continuity, crowding perception, socialization and bonding, and the social group as the primary behaving unit—make the greatest contribution to the larger interest of rural sociology and sociology in general.

It may be useful to consider some of the characteristics of studies in the four areas. Studies on continuity in social values

(Machlis, 1975; Burch, 1965; West and Merriam, 1970) tend to concentrate on family units in wildland settings, usually camping. However, there are some studies that track value continuity within a particular activity (Bryan, 1977), whereas Field and Cheek (1974) and their colleagues have given considerable attention to participants other than family members.

Studies of crowding perceptions and social carrying capacity of wildlands have been something of a cottage industry for rural sociologists and others. In addition to helping supplement faculty salaries, the sheer magnitude of data has given us real insight into how to measure "satisfaction" (Heberlein, 1977) and the sociological factors affecting satisfaction (Shelby, et al., 1983). Researchers have been much more directly involved with policy (Stankey and McCool, 1984). And, like studies of wildland deviation, there has been much concern with moral choices (Bultena, et al., 1981). Finally, issues of the nature of group and individual solitude and the role that spacing and territoriality play in sustaining such patterns have been given theoretical (Burch, 1981) and empirical examination (Lee, 1977).

Studies on socialization, recreation behavior, and social bonding have directly tested the developmental aspects of socialization (Kelly, 1974; Yoesting and Burkhead, 1973; Sofranko and Nolan 1972) and the importance of recreation settings for social bonding (Klessig and Hale, 1972). Cheek and Burch (1976:121) summarize the importance of such studies when they note that

the consistency of these associations found across a broad range of studies, regions, activities, cultures, and times suggest social regularities of more than passing interest. Might it be that our grand and elaborate theories of social change and stability have unduly favored the drama of work, war and rational order over the mundane trivia of non-work, life cycle forces, and the emotional order of primary associations?

Rural sociologists have long made the family farmer a center of interest and emotional commitment, even when, as we noted earlier, they are no longer the major productive units of agriculture. Yet, wildland studies have found that the small social group is the major wildland recreation behavioral unit (Field and O'Leary, 1973; Dottavio, et al., 1980; Burch, 1969). They have also fit wildland recreation into a larger class and work system (Cheek, 1971; Burdge, 1969), yet, the primary source of meaning remains the small group (Buchanan, et al., 1981; Field and O'Leary, 1973). Indeed, as Field, et al. (1985:1) argue, there is an essential "interplay of human culture, social groups, and natural resource systems in defining human behavior at a recreation site." Their work reaffirms what over two decades of research has demonstrated: there must be a congruence of biophysical factors, a particular kind of group structure and a certain value or management orientation in order to produce a particular social output. In recreation as in agriculture such outputs are both regular and predictable.

Studies of Environmental Concern as a Social Movement

Our second major category of natural resources sociology is the extensive work done on environmentalism as a social movement. We group these studies into four general areas—value trends, organizational trends, social class trends, and trends in public opinion.

Studies of value trends consider how one set of concerns such as civil rights led to participation in the environmental movement (Gale, 1972) or how outdoor recreation participation is associated with environmental concern (Dunlap and Heffernan, 1975). Other studies examine how the various demographic factors such as age, level of educational attainment, place of residence, and so forth affect the nature and types of concern (Dillman and Christenson, 1974; Buttel and Flinn, 1974). And some studies note the interactive influence between a particular agency and changes in the movement (Gale, 1986).

Organizational studies focus more directly on the movement itself and permit us to see an evolution from general public concern to ever more sophisticated political pressure groups (Morrison, et al., 1972; Schnaiberg, 1973; Faich and Gale, 1971). Other studies describe the changing nature of supporters as some goals are accomplished and as the media attention changes (Dunlap and Dillman, 1976; Buttel and Larson, 1980; Dunlap and Gale, 1972; Heberlein, 1972).

Social class has always been an important variable in sociological explanations. Yet, in recreation studies class position is a very poor predictor of the nature and amount of recreation activity chosen. In recreation, class has been more a general constraint on opportunity. This turn-around on a favorite variable has had similar patterns in the studies of environmentalism. There has been a strong interest in demonstrating the upper-class aspects of environmentalism (Harry, et al., 1969; Hendee, et al., 1969; Devall, 1970). However, equally strong studies have found a broader base of support (McEvoy, 1971; McEvoy, 1972; Mitchell, 1979). Of particular interest have been the several studies interested in the association between distributional patterns and lifestyles (Morrison, 1976, 1986; Mazur and Rosa, 1974). These latter studies have used an underlying interest in equity issues to develop greater theoretical comprehensiveness than simple hypotheses regarding class associations. In short, the greater complexity of behavioral determinants is being given orderly form and testing (Van Liere and Dunlap, 1980).

Finally, a large group of studies has been done in the traditional areas of public opinion polling and the general recording of trends and patterns in opinion polls. These studies are no different than studies on farmers attitudes toward certain kinds of price support programs; they simply ask a broader population about environmental matters (Gabbard and Coughenour, 1973; Dillman and Christenson, 1972). Others attempt to identify the factors affecting the observed trends in opinion (O'Riordan, 1971; Means, 1972; Orr, 1974; Buttel, 1975; Morrison, 1980). These latter studies treat opinion formation as a form of behavior rather than using opinions as measures or predictors of likely future behavior.

Environmentalism Influences on Theory Development

A third problem loci has been stimulated by environmental quality concerns. P. J. Richerson and J. McEvoy (1976) and

Burch and DeLuca (1984) are interested in developing a human ecology that is drawn from or is more part of ongoing theory development in biological ecology. Catton and Dunlap's (1978) notion of a shift from the "human exceptionalism paradigm" (HEP) to the "new environmental paradigm" (NEP) is one example of a theoretical approach responding to a felt crisis; whereas Buttel's (1978) challenges and Schnaibergs' (1980) approach respond to the crisis from a more traditional Marxian and Weberian paradigm. Though the debate has been concerned with the appropriateness and utility of respective paradigms it seems more reflective of the fact that most environmental sociology research in the 1960s and early 1970s had a wildland venue. Therefore, in spite of much being said about man as part of nature, most of the research was applied to regions with the least human effect. Indeed, there was a clear spatial separation, such that parks and wilderness areas were treated as more ideal places of sociality than were the rural and urban settlements left behind.

The environmental movement was seen as primarily driven by the same passion as that for wildland aesthetics and recreational solitude. The movement seemed to be more focused on lifestyle than about past concerns over wages and working conditions. Consequently, unlike the early ecological, rural sociology studies, the paradigms derived from wildland recreation, and aesthetics did not link humanity to nature through the essential *processes of production*, but rather made nature an object of diversion or sacred contemplation. In a sense, *processes of consumption* rather than *processes of production* became the link to nature. The HEP-NEP debate naturally followed those patterns shaped by the predominant empirical and applied research findings. As the venue for a greater and greater proportion of empirical and applied research shifts from wildlands to community forestry projects in the tropics, or to site planning for toxic waste management, or to the assessment of timber-cutting impacts on local communities, the emerging paradigms then are more likely to reflect something of the earlier attention to productive processes as the link between society and nature.

Two other influences have been those of biologists attempting to rewrite human ecology. These have been political ecologists such as D. H. Meadows and D. L. Meadows (1974), W. C. Paddock and P. Paddock (1967), G. Hardin (1974), P. Ehrlich (1985), and their various students and fellow travelers. Such approaches have been neo-Malthusian and essentially anti-human, yet their lifeboat ethics have influenced many rural sociologists to rethink and restate their humanist perspectives. While Barry Commoner (1977) and his colleagues gave less attention to the fashionable ecological gloom of their biological colleagues by emphasizing sociological aspects of equity and distribution, solutions were clearly within the social rather than biological realm.

An even more positive influence came from the studies of animal behaviorists and ethologists such as L. Tiger and R. Fox (1971), and H. Kummer (1971). In the 1970s, papers on the social behavior of wolves, dairy cows, and macaques mingled with usual ones on wilderness, carrying capacity, and forestry communities at the NRRG sessions of the Rural Sociological Society. These students brought to the meetings clearer methods of observation, better description and use of primary variables, and new ways to consider the role of genetics and suggested ways in which cross-species studies could advance a biocentric human ecology. In short, as we noted at the outset, the NRRG was the venue for creating a more ecologically aware theory of human social behavior and developing the unique techniques of measurement such theory development requires.

Urban-Industrial Influences

As the reader will note, the major problem loci of natural resources sociology have a clear thread of continuity with traditional interests of rural sociology. Indeed, they grow out of, retransform, and thereby become a new synthesis of traditional practices and approaches. For example, rural sociology has always had a strong tinge of moral concern for the rural people and the rural way of life. Rural sociologists wanted churches to thrive and trading communities to prosper and for young people to have "responsible" sex lives and to avoid alcoholism and other vices. The environmentalism of the natural resource sociologist has an equally strong tinge of moral concern, of a world and a way of life about to be lost, unless certain "scientifically" discovered practices are adopted.

There is a similar continuity and patterning within the natural resource work too. For example, nearly all of the work that passes under the heading of social impact assessment was anticipated, though not called SIA, by early concerns about technological influences on rural social systems. When we look at the studies in the problem loci we call urban-industrial influences we find consistent patterns of continuity from extremely diverse areas of study focus. There is a common thread of interest in urban structure such as the distribution of power, value, and land use. Walter Firey (1947), a rural sociologist, brilliantly analyzes how values override economics in a study of land use in Boston. A journalist and social psychologist William F. Whyte (1968) examines the pressures on rural landscape values by urban sprawl. An urban sociologist Herbert Gans (1962, 1967) examines that very sprawl after examining how urban folk behave like rural villagers.

Later, the political sociologist Delbert Miller (1972) examines how urban leaders value environmental issues, while in an early study, Phillip Selznick (1949) examines how interest groups influenced a major governmental agency that was to help rural development. Finally, a wide range of studies cluster around power and its exertion in environmental matters such as oil spills (Molotch 1970), left-right political divisions (Buttel and Flinn 1976; Schnaiberg, 1980), and the political consequences of limits to growth (Catton and Dunlap 1980).

The main point here is that well before the environmental decade of the 1960s, there were systematic investigations of man-environment relations, and those investigations should be part of the cumulative research memory of natural resources sociology. This linkage may be clearest in the studies of the technological impact on social systems. To take an arbitrary starting point we have Mumford's (1934) classic study of technology; later there is Cottrell's (1951) study of a town impacted when a railroad goes from steam to diesel. This served as a test of what eventually grew into his *Energy and Society* (1955), a book that clearly anticipated the key variables and the likely consequences of high-technological–high-energy systems in the rural development of developing countries and elsewhere. A whole series of studies considered the impact of industrialization on rural areas (Field, 1968; Bertrand and Osborne, 1959; Hoffer and Freeman, 1955; Breese, et al. 1965), while these seeds of theory and analysis were anticipated by volumes such as W. Thomas' *Man's Role in Changing the Face of the Earth* (1956). Studies of forced residential relocation due to reservoir construction (Burdge and Ludtke, 1972) were the lineal antecedents of K. Finsterbusch and C. P. Wolf (1980) and Burch and DeLuca (1984) on social impact assessment. The next stage of concern is likely to be found in studies on the impact of biotechnology on the third world rural communities (Buttel, et al., 1985) and the more applied forms of human ecology (Murdock, 1979; Wolf, 1986) that are emerging from SIA specialists.

This pattern is equally clear in the spatial analyses conducted by scholars in the late 1960s and early 1970s who were looking at the influences of the physical environment on observed regularities of behavior (Zeisel, 1975). Indeed, their approaches and findings are not unlike those of other rural sociologists who looked at the spatial aspects of rural settlements (Zimmerman, 1930; Zimmerman and Moneo, 1971; Hodge, 1966; Young and Larson, 1970). The difference is that these 1960s scholars were considering the built environment of cities, suburbs, and structured spaces such as rooms and offices.

There was Walter Firey's (1945) early report on the social meaning of space, followed by Edward Hall's (1966) influential, *The Hidden Dimension*. Roger Barker (1968) and his colleagues developed a means for analyzing how an entire small town used its space. Robert Sommer (1969) moved inside to look at the status and determinants of design features on human behavior, while Kevin Lynch (1960) and his colleagues considered how people cognitively mapped or failed to map certain urban locales. William Michelson (1970) provided an amazing summary of all the non-economic influences on spatial behavior in human society. Robert Lee (1973) examined how a wide range of potentially incompatible groups could be in close approximation without conflict because they had clearly established spatial territories. Lee's (1973) work and the work of others (e.g., Cheek, et al., 1976; Jobes, 1976) illustrate how these approaches, theories and methods were adopted in some form, either directly or indirectly in guiding natural resources research on wildlands and rural areas.

CONCLUSION AND SUGGESTIONS FOR NEW DIRECTIONS

We have greatly condensed the ideas and findings from a period of tremendous growth and diversity by natural resources sociology. However, we have demonstrated how specialization around certain resource issues has expanded the domain of rural sociology. We clustered our observations of the research around four broad loci of influence—wildlands, environmentalism as a social movement, environmentalism influences on theory development, and urban-industrial influences. Within these broad loci of influence we attempted to identify what we think have been the major contributions to understanding social behavior relative to natural resources.

Under wildlands we considered how studies have demonstrated regular influences between resource developments and predictable outcomes in community stability and change. We considered how studies on woods-burning and depreciative behavior in recreation settings have given us a clearer understanding of the nature, sources, and sanction effects of moral norms. Wildland institutional studies have confirmed how certain developments have predictable impact on certain social institutions; how regularities of distributional institutions affect the costs and benefits of resources and pollution, and how the property rights and gender role institutions affect conservation practices. We concluded the wildlands section by considering the range of findings in the largest body of research—small group behavior in wildland settings. We found substantial support for the importance of wildlands in establishing and maintaining value continuity between generations. Studies on crowding perception and carrying capacity demonstrate that perception is filtered by the values of intimate social groups rather than a direct physical response. Studies on socialization and social bonding gave clarity to our understanding of such processes. And finally the preeminence of the intimate social group as the primary behaving unit in wildland recreation settings establishes the saliency of cultural and social organizational factors in defining human habitats.

The second major loci of influence considered how environmentalism fits as a social movement process. These studies considered how the movement was evolving in values and organizational structure as part of a natural process. There were a large number of studies on the class basis of the movement, however, like recreation, the cross-trends suggested more complex determinants. Finally, there was a continuation of rural sociological interest in public opinion trends but with a shift to a new set of issues.

Our third loci of influence emphasized an earlier discussion of how environmentalism was changing our perceptions, such that new kinds of theoretical explanation and measures were being required. The fourth major loci of influence considered how urban-industrial studies led from traditional spatial interests of rural sociologists right back to natural resource sociology interests. We considered the importance of power and its exercise and traced how an early interest in technological influences lead to current interests in environmental impact assessment.

We have suggested that within the confines of rural sociology there has been a tremendous diversity of issues and approaches in the development of a natural resource sociology, yet there has also been a consistent clustering around a few key issues. For example, Burch and Wade (1985) examined twenty years of natural resources sociology in the RSS by counting the nature and types of papers presented at the annual RSS meetings. They found not only a steady growth in the number of sessions and the number of environmentally oriented papers presented, but a definite pattern of concentration. They found that through 1984, 21.9 percent of the papers have been on wildland recreation, 20.8 percent on environmental impact; 10.7 percent on energy and society issues, and 8 percent on the environmental movement itself.

Yet when we consider the spreading domain of influence by the rural sociological natural resource folk we see they have contributed much to theory, methods, and data for examining wide issues of environmental importance just as they have gained an equally large amount from other domains of interest. Certainly, the large bulk of empirical findings were produced in this era—so the domain of these studies expanded and the very data base itself made an exponential rise. Natural resource sociology had come of empirical age, though there were significant doubts about the capacity of its theory to manage all the data.

REFERENCES

General

Brown, Lester. 1975. "The world food prospect." *Science* 190:1053–1059.

Burch, William R., Jr., and Jerry L. Wade. 1985. "Through the glass darkly: twenty years of natural resource sociology." The *Rural Sociologist* 5:89–95.

Campbell, Rex R., and Jerry L. Wade, (eds.). 1972. *Society and Environment: The Coming Collision.* Boston: Allyn and Bacon.

Ehrlich, Paul. 1985. "Human ecology for introductory biology courses: an overview." *American Zoologist* 25:379–394.

Hardin, Garrett. 1974. "Lifeboat ethics: the case against helping the poor." *Psychology Today* 8:38–43, 123–126.

Hirst, E. 1974. "Food-related energy requirements." *Science* 184:132–138.

Jensen, Neal F. 1978. "Limits to growth in world food production." *Science* 201:317–320.

Kellert, Stephen. 1982. "Conceptual framework for explaining attitudes toward western energy development impacts on wildlife and related findings." In *Proceedings of a National Symposium on Issues and Technology in the Management of Impacted Western Wildlife*, 169–178. Steamboat Springs, Colorado: Thorne, Ecological Institute.

Loomis, Charles P. 1960. *Social Systems.* New York: D. Van Nostrand.

Meadows, Donella H., Dennis L. Meadows, Jorgen Randers, and William W. Behrens III. 1974. *The Limits to Growth.* New York: Universe.

Merton, Robert K. 1968. *Social Theory and Social Structure*. New York: Free Press.

Paddock, William C., and Paul Paddock. 1967. *Famine 1975!* Boston: Little, Brown.

Parsons, Talcott. 1951. *The Social System*. Glencoe, Illinois: Free Press.

Pimentel, D., L. E. Hurd, A. C. Belloti, M. J. Forster, et al. 1973. "Food production and the energy crisis." *Science* 182:443–449.

Richerson, Peter J., and James McEvoy III. 1976. *Human Ecology: An Environmental Approach*. North Scituate, Massachusetts: Duxbury Press.

Schertz, P. Lyle et al. 1979. "Farming in the United States." *Structure Issues of American Agriculture*. Washington, D.C.: U.S. Department of Agriculture, Economics, Statistics and Cooperatives Service Agricultural Economic Report No. 438, 24–42.

Spaulding, Irving A. 1986. *Rural-Urban Ratios Handbook United States: 1790–1980*. Kingston: University of Rhode Island Agricultural Experiment Station Contribution No. 2314.

Steinhart, J. S., and C. E. Steinhart. 1974. "Energy use in the U.S. food system." *Science* 184:307–316.

Theory—From Human Ecology to Social Ecology

Burch, William R., Jr., and Donald R. DeLuca. 1984. *Measuring the Social Impact of Natural Resource Policies*. Albuquerque: University of New Mexico Press.

Burch, William R., Jr. 1971. *Daydreams and Nightmares: A Sociological Essay on the American Environment*. New York: Harper & Row.

Buttel, Frederick H. 1978. "Environmental sociology: a new paradigm?" *The American Sociologist* 13:41–49.

Catton, William R., Jr., and Riley E. Dunlap. 1978. "Environmental sociology: a new paradigm." *The American Sociologist* 13:252–256.

Catton, William R., Jr., and Riley E. Dunlap. 1980. "A new ecological paradigm for post-exuberant sociology." *American Behavioral Scientist*. 24:15–47.

Ehrlich, Paul. 1985. "Human ecology for introductory biology courses: an overview." *American Zoologist* 25:379–394.

Firey, Walter. 1960. *Man, Mind and Land*. Glencoe, Illinois: The Free Press.

Kummer, Hans. 1971. *Primate Societies*. Chicago: Aldine.

McEvoy, James III. 1972. "The American concern with the environment." In *Social Behavior, Natural Resources and the Environment*, ed. William R. Burch, Jr., Neil H. Cheek, Jr., and Lee Taylor, 214–236. New York: Harper and Row.

Rosa, Eugene A., and Gary E. Machlis. 1985. "Energetic theories of society: an evaluative review." *Sociological Inquiry* 53:152–178.

Tiger, Lionel, and Robin Fox. 1971. *The Imperial Animal*. New York: Holt, Rinehart and Winston.

Methods—Observation

Burch, William R., Jr. 1964. *A New Look at an Old Friend—Observation as a Technique for Recreation Research*. Portland, Oregon: USDA/USFS Pacific Northwest Forest and Range Experiment Station Research Paper.

Burch, William R., Jr. 1965. "The play world of camping, research into the social meaning of outdoor recreation." *American Journal of Sociology* 70:604–612.

James, G. A., and H. T. Schreuder. 1972. *Estimating Dispersed Recreation Use along Trails and in General Undeveloped Areas with Electric-Eye Counters: Some Preliminary Findings*. USDA Forest Service Research Note SE-181. Atlanta: South Eastern Forest and Range Experiment Station.

Lee, Robert G. 1975. *The Management of Human Components in the Yosemite National Park Ecosystem: Final Research Report*. Berkeley: University of California, Department of Forestry and Conservation.

Love, L. D. 1964. *Summer Recreational Use of Selected National Forest Campgrounds in the Central Rocky Mountains*. USDA Forest Service Research Paper RM-5. Fort Collins, Colorado: Rocky Mountain Forest and Range Experiment Station.

Methods—Historical Comparison

Burch, William R., Jr. 1971. *Daydreams and Nightmares: A Sociological Essay on the American Environment*. New York: Harper and Row.

Cottrell, Frederick. 1955. *Energy and Society*. New York: McGraw Hill Inc.

Duncan, Otis Dudley. 1964. "Social organization and the ecosystem." In *Handbook of Modern Sociology*, ed. Robert Farris, 36–82. Chicago: Rand McNally.

Schnaiberg, Allan. 1980. *The Environment: From Surplus to Scarcity.* New York: Oxford University Press.

Methods—Cross-Species Comparisons

Burch, William R., Jr. 1976. "The peregrine falcon and the urban poor: some sociological interpretations." In *Human Ecology: An Environmental Approach,* ed. Peter J. Richerson and James McEvoy III, 308–316. North Scituate, Massachusetts: Duxbury Press.

Cheek, Neil H., Jr. 1972. "Aspects of social age." Paper presented at the Rural Sociological Society annual meeting, San Francisco.

Cheek, Neil H., Jr., and William R. Burch, Jr. 1976. *The Social Organization of Leisure in Human Society.* New York: Harper & Row.

Crook, John Hurrell. 1970. "The social ecology of primates." In *Social Behavior in Birds and Mammals,* ed. J. H. Crook, 103–166. New York: Academic Press.

Dolhinow, Phyllis. 1971. "At play in the fields." *Natural History* 81:66–71.

Tiger, Lionel. 1969. *Men in Groups.* New York: Random House.

Methods—Public Policy Survey

Burdge, Rabel J. 1982. "Needs assessment surveys for decision makers." In *Rural Society in the U.S.: Research Issues for the 1980s,* ed. Don A. Dillman and Daryl J. Hobbs, 273–283. Boulder, Colorado: Westview Press.

Dillman, Don A. 1971. *Public Values and Concerns of Washington Residents.* Pullman: Washington Agricultural Experiment Station Bulletin No. 748.

Wenner, Lambert. 1985. *Social Science Information and Resource Management.* Washington, D.C.: USDA Forest Service.

Methods—Field Experiments

Clark, Roger N., John C. Hendee, and Robert L. Burgess. 1972. "The experimental control of littering." *Journal of Environmental Education.* 4:22–28.

Heberlein, Thomas. 1971. "Moral norms, threatened sanctions, and littering behavior." Ph.D. thesis, University of Wisconsin, Madison.

Heberlein, Thomas. 1975. "Conservation information: the energy cri-
    sis and electricity consumption in an apartment complex." *En-
    ergy Systems and Policy* 1:105–18.

Methods—Perception and Valuation

Bultena, Gordon L., and John C. Hendee. 1972. "Foresters' views of
    interest group positions on forest policy." *Journal of Forestry*
    70:337–342.
Capener, Harold R. 1973. *Perceptions of Environmental Quality Prob-
    lems in the Hudson River Region.* Ithaca: New York State Col-
    lege of Agriculture and Life Sciences, Department of Rural
    Sociology.
Ditton, R. B., A. J. Fedler, and A. R. Graefe. 1982. "Assessing recre-
    ational satisfaction among diverse participant groups." In *For-
    est and River Recreation: Research Update*, 134–139. St. Paul:
    University of Minnesota Agricultural Experiment Station Bul-
    letin No. 18.
Herberlein, Thomas. 1974. "The three fixes: technological, cognitive,
    and structural." In *Water and Community Development: Social
    and Economic Perspectives*, ed. Donald R. Field, James C. Bar-
    ron, and Burl F. Long, 279–295. Ann Arbor, Michigan: Ann
    Arbor Science.
Heberlein, Thomas, J. N. Trent, and R. M. Baumgartner. 1982. "The
    influence of hunter density on fire arm deer hunters' satisfac-
    tion: a field experiment." *Transactions of the Forty-Seventh
    North American Wildlife and Natural Resource Conference*
    47:665–676.
Lee, Robert G. 1976. "The social definition of outdoor recreation
    places." In *Leisure and Recreation Places*, ed. Neil H. Cheek,
    Jr., Donald R. Field, and Rabel J. Burdge, 31–45. Ann Arbor,
    Michigan: Ann Arbor Press.
Peterson, George L. 1974. "Evaluating the quality of the wilderness
    environment: congruence between perception and aspiration."
    Environment and Behavior 6:169–193.
Schreyer, R., and J. W. Roggenbuck. 1981. "Visitor images of national
    parks: the influence of social definitions of places on perceptions
    and behavior." In *Some Recent Products of River Recreation
    Research*, 39–44. St. Paul, Minnesota: USDA Forest Service
    General Technical Report WC-63.

Wildlands

Community Stability and Change and Resource Development

Andrews, Wade H., and Dennis C. Geersten. 1970. *The Function of Social Behavior in Water Resource Development.* Logan: Utah State University, Institute for Social Science Research on Natural Resources Research Report 1.

Baird, Andrew W. 1965. *Attitudes and Characteristics of Forest Residents in Three Mississippi Counties.* State College: Mississippi State University, Social Science Research Center Preliminary Report No. 8.

Barth, Fredrick. 1959. "Subsistence and institutional system in a Norwegian mountain valley." *Rural Sociology* 17:28–38.

Fruedenburg, William. 1984. "Boomtown's youth: the differential impacts of rapid community growth on adolescents and adults." *American Sociological Review* 49:697–705.

Gibson, D. C. 1944. *Socio-economic Evolution in Timbered Area in Northern Michigan—A Case Study of Sheboygon, Michigan, 1890–1940.* East Lansing: Michigan State College Agricultural Experiment Station Technical Bulletin No. 193.

Goldschmidt, Walter. 1978. *As You Sow: Three Studies in the Social Consequences of Agribusiness.* Montclair, New Jersey: Allanheld, Osburn.

Graber, Edith E. 1974. "Newcomers and oldtimers: growth and change in a mountain town." *Rural Sociology* 39:504–513.

Kaufman, Harold F. 1939. "Social factors in the reforestation of the Missouri Ozarks." M.A. thesis, University of Missouri, Columbia.

Kaufman, Harold F. 1961. "The forest and community planning." State College: Mississippi State University Agricultural Experiment Station, Sociology and Rural Life.

Knowlton, Clark. 1972. "Culture conflict and natural resources." In *Social Behavior, Natural Resources and the Environment,* ed. William R. Burch, Jr., Neil Cheek, Jr., and Lee Taylor, 109–146. New York: Harper & Row.

Lee, Robert G. 1985. "Comparative analysis of stability in forest dependent communities of Japan and the Pacific Northwest United States." Paper presented at the Rural Sociological Association annual meeting, Blacksburg, Virginia.

Voland, Maurice E., and William Fleischman. 1982. *Sociology and*

    Social Impact Analysis in the Federal Natural Resource Management Agencies. Washington, D.C.: USDA Forest Service.

Wenner, Lambert. 1984. *Issues in Social Impact Analysis: Proceedings from an Interagency Symposium*. Washington, D.C.: USDA Forest Service.

Wilkinson, Kenneth P., and Peyton A. Hughes. 1966. "Community Factors in Watershed development." In *Proceedings of the Mississippi Water Resources Conference*, 24–32. State College: Mississippi State University Water Resources Institute.

Deviation

Baird, Andrew W. 1969. *Rural Residents and Forest Fire Risk: Guides to Forest Fire Prevention*. State College: Mississippi State University, Social Science Research Center Report No. 28.

Campbell, F. L., John C. Hendee, and Roger Clark. 1968. "Law and order in public parks." *Parks and Recreation* 3:28–33, 51–55.

Clark, Roger N., John C. Hendee, and Robert L. Burgess. 1972. "The experimental control of littering." *Journal of Environmental Education* 4:22–28.

Doolittle, Max L. 1972. "Planning fire prevention communications." *Journal of Forestry* 70:607–609.

Fahnestock, George R. 1964. *Southern Forest Fires: A Social Challenge*. New Orleans: U.S. Forest Service Southern Forest Experiment Station, Preliminary Report No. 2.

Folkman, William S. 1972. "Studying the people who cause forest fires." In *Social Behavior, Natural Resources and the Environment*, ed. William R. Burch, Jr., Neil H. Cheek, Jr., and Lee Taylor, 44–64. New York: Harper & Row.

Heberlein, Thomas. 1971. "Moral norms, threatened sanctions, and littering behavior." Ph.D. thesis, University of Wisconsin, Madison.

Heffernan, William D., and G. Dale Welch. 1972. "Latent deviancy and social interaction: the willful destruction of natural resources." In *Social Behavior, Natural Resources and the Environment*, ed. William R. Burch, Jr., Neil H. Cheek, Jr., and Lee Taylor, 174–184. New York: Harper & Row.

Jones, Arthur R., Jr., M. Lee Taylor, and Alvin L. Bertrand. 1965. *Some Human Factors in Woods Burning*. Baton Rouge: Louisiana State University Agricultural Experiment Station Bulletin No. 601.

Development

Johnson, Sue, and Rabel J. Burdge. 1974. "An analysis of community and individual reactions to foreign migration due to reservoir construction." In *Water and Community Development: Social and Economic Perspectives,* ed. Donald R. Field, James C. Barron, and Burl F. Long, 169–196. Ann Arbor, Michigan: Ann Arbor Science.

Photiadis, John D. 1960. *Attitudes Toward the Water Resources Development Program in Central South Dakota.* Brookings: South Dakota State University, Department of Rural Sociology Extension Service and Water Resources Commission, Preliminary Report No. 1.

Singh, Raghu N., and Kenneth P. Wilkinson. 1974. "On the measurement of environmental impacts of public projects from a sociological perspective." *Water Resources Bulletin* 10:415–425.

Distribution of Costs and Benefits

Field, Donald R., and Neil H. Cheek, Jr. 1974. "A basis for assessing differential participation in water-based recreation." *Water Resources Bulletin* 10:1218–1227.

Humphrey, Craig R., and Frederick R. Buttel. 1982. *Environment, Energy, and Society.* Belmont, California: Wadsworth.

Institute for Social Science Research on Natural Resources. 1968. *Proceedings of the Workshop for Sociological Aspects of Water Resources Research.* Logan: Utah State University.

Schnaiberg, Allan. 1975. "Social synthesis of the societal-environmental dialectic: the role of distributional impacts." *Social Science Quarterly* 56:5–20.

Spaulding, Irving A. 1972. "Social class and household water consumption." In *Social Behavior, Natural Resources and the Environment,* ed. William R. Burch, Jr., Neil H. Cheek, Jr., and Lee Taylor, 11–28. New York: Harper & Row.

Property Rights

Ashby, Jacqueline, A. 1985. "The social ecology of soil erosion in a Columbian farming system." *Rural Sociology* 50:377–396.

Fortmann, Louise. 1985a. "The tree tenure factor in agroforestry with particular reference to Africa." *Agroforestry Systems* 2:229–251.

Tarver, James D. 1963. "Ecological patterns of land tenure, farm land uses, and farm population characteristics." *Rural Sociology* 28:128–145.

West, Patrick C. 1982. *Natural Resource Bureaucracy and Rural Poverty: A Study in the Political Sociology of Natural Resources.* Ann Arbor: University of Michigan Natural Resources Sociology Research Lab Monograph No. 2.

Gender Roles

Buttel, Frederick, H., and Gilbert W. Gillespie, Jr. 1984. "The sexual division of farm household labor: an exploratory study of the structure of on-farm and off-farm allocation among farm men and women." *Rural Sociology* 49:183–209.

Fortmann, Louise, and Dianne Rocheleau. 1985. "Women and agroforestry: four myths and three case studies." *Agroforestry Systems* 2:253–272.

Hoskins, Marilyn W. 1979. *Women in Forestry for Local Community Development: A Programming Guide.* Washington, D.C.: Agency for International Development Report No. AID–OTR–147–79–83.

Williams, Paula. 1983. "The social organization of firewood procurement and use in Africa: a study of the division of labor by sex." Ph.D. dissertation, University of Washington, Seattle.

Groups in Recreation—Continuity in Social Values and Wildland Recreation Settings

Bryan, Hobson. 1977. "Leisure value systems and recreational specialization: the case of trout fishermen." *Journal of Leisure Research* 9:174–187.

Burch, William R., Jr. 1965. "The play world of camping: research into the social meaning of outdoor recreation." *American Journal of Sociology* 70:604–612.

Field, Donald R., and Neil H. Cheek, Jr. 1974. "A basis for assessing differential participation in water-oriented recreation." *Water Resources Bulletin* 10:1218–1227.

Machlis, Gary E. 1975. "Families in parks: an analysis of family organization in a leisure setting." M.S. thesis, University of Washington, Seattle.

West, Patrick C., and Larry C. Merriam. 1970. "Outdoor recreation and family cohesiveness: a research approach." *Journal of Leisure Research* 2:251–259.

Perceptions of Crowding and the Social Carrying Capacity of Wildland Recreation Settings

Bultena, Gordon L., D. Albrecht, and Peter Womble. 1981. "Freedom versus control: a study of backpackers preferences for wilderness management." *Leisure Sciences* 4:297–310.

Burch, William R., Jr. 1981. "The ecology of metaphor—spacing regularities for humans and other primates in urban and wildland habitats." *Leisure Sciences* 4:213–231.

Heberlein, Thomas. 1977. "Density, crowding, and satisfaction: sociological studies for determining carrying capacities." In *Proceedings: River Recreation Management and Research Symposium*, 67–76. USDA Forest Service General Technical Report NC-28.

Lee, Robert G. 1977. "Alone with others: the paradox of privacy in wilderness." *Leisure Sciences* 1:3–19.

Shelby, Bo, Thomas Heberlein, J. J. Vaske, and G. Alfano. 1983. "Expectations, preferences, and feeling crowded in recreation activities." *Leisure Sciences* 6:1–14.

Stankey, George H., and Stephen F. McCool. 1984. "Carrying capacity in recreational settings: evaluation, appraisal, and application." *Leisure Sciences* 6:453–473.

Socialization, Recreation Behavior, and Social Bonding in Wildland Settings

Cheek, Neil H., Jr. and William R. Burch, Jr. 1976. *The Social Organization of Leisure in Human Society*. New York: Harper & Row.

Kelly, John R. 1974. "Socialization toward leisure, a developmental approach." *Journal of Leisure Research* 6:181–193.

Klessig, Lowell, and James B. Hale. 1972. *A Profile of Wisconsin Hunters*. Madison, Wisconsin: Department of Natural Resources Technical Bulletin No. 60.

Sofranko, Andrew J., and Michael F. Nolan. 1972. "Early life experiences and adult sports participation." *Journal of Leisure Research* 4:6–18.

Yoesting, Dean R., and Dan L. Burkhead. 1973. "Significance of childhood recreation experience on adult leisure behavior, an exploratory analysis." *Journal of Leisure Research* 5:25–36.

Social Group as Primary Behavioral Unit in Wildland Recreation Places

Buchanan, T., J. E. Christiansen, and R. J. Burdge. 1981. "Social groups and the meaning of outdoor recreation activities." *Journal of Leisure Research* 13:254–266.

Burch, William R., Jr. 1969. "The social circles of leisures competing explanations." *Journal of Leisure Research* 1:125–147.

Burdge, Rabel J. 1969. "Levels of occupational prestige and leisure activity." *Journal of Leisure Research* 9:262–274.

Cheek, Neil H. 1971. "Toward a sociology of not-work." *Pacific Sociological Review* 14:245–258.

Dottavio, F. D., Joseph O'Leary, and Barbara Koth. 1980. "The social group variable in recreation participation studies." *Journal of Leisure Research* 12:357–367.

Field, Donald R., Martha E. Lee, and Kristen Martinson. 1985. "Human behavior and recreation habitats: conceptual issues." In *Riparian Ecosystems and Their Management*, ed. Roy Johnson, 227–231. U.S. Forest Service, General Technical Report Rm. 120. Fort Collins, Colorado: Rocky Mountain Forest and Range Experimentation.

Field, Donald R., and Joseph T. O'Leary. 1973. "Social groups as a basis for assessing participation in selected water activities." *Journal of Leisure Research* 5:16–25.

Manning, Robert E. 1986. *Studies in Outdoor Recreation Search and Research for Satisfaction*. Corvallis: Oregon State University Press.

Environmentalism as a Social Movement

Value Trends

Buttel, Frederick H., and William L. Flinn. 1974. "The structure of support for the environmental movement, 1968–1970." *Rural Sociology* 39:56–69.

Dillman, Don A., and James A. Christenson. 1974. "Toward the assessment of public values." *Public Opinion Quarterly* 38:206–221.

Dunlap, Riley E., and Robert Bruce Heffernan. 1975. "Outdoor recreation and environmental concern: an empirical examination." *Rural Sociology* 40:18–30.

Gale, Richard P. 1972. "From sit-in to hike-in: a comparison of the civil rights and environmental movements." In *Social Behavior, Natural Resources and the Environment*, ed. William R. Burch, Jr., Neil H. Cheek, Jr., and Lee Taylor, 280–305. New York: Harper & Row.

Gale, Richard P. 1986. "The U.S. Forest Service and the evolution of the environmental movement." *Western Wildlands* 11:22–26.

Organizational Trends

Buttel, Frederick H., and Oscar W. Larson III. 1980. "Whither environmentalism? The future political path of the environmental movement." *Natural Resources Journal* 20:323–344.

Dunlap, Riley E., and Don A. Dillman. 1976. "Decline in public support for environmental protection: evidence from a 1970–1974 panel study." *Rural Sociology* 41:382–390.

Dunlap, Riley E., and Richard P. Gale. 1972. "Politics and ecology: a political profile of student eco-activists." *Youth and Society* 3:379–397.

Faich, Ronald G., and Richard P. Gale. 1971. "The environmental movement: from recreation to politics." *Pacific Sociological Review* 14:270–287.

Heberlein, Thomas. 1972. "A land ethic realized; some social psychological explanations for changing environmental attitudes." *Journal of Social Issues* 28:79–87.

Morrison, Denton E., Kenneth E. Hornback, and W. Keith Warner. 1972. "The environmental movement: some preliminary observations and predictions." In *Social Behavior, Natural Resources and the Environment*, ed. William R. Burch, Jr., Neil Cheek, Jr., and Lee Taylor, 254–279. New York: Harper & Row.

Schnaiberg, Allan. 1973. "Politics, participation, and pollution: the environmental movement." In *Cities in Change: A Reader and Urban Sociology*, ed. J. Walton and D. Earns, 605–627. Boston: Allyn and Bacon.

Social Class Trends

Devall, William B. 1970. "Conservation: an upper-middle class social movement: a replication." *Journal of Leisure Research* 2:123–126.

Dunlap, Riley E., and William R. Catton, Jr. 1979. "Environmental Sociology." *Annual Review of Sociology* 5:243–273.

Harry, Joseph, Richard P. Gale, and John C. Hendee. 1969. "Conservation: an upper-middle class social movement." *Journal of Leisure Research* 1:246–254.

Harry, Joseph, Richard P. Gale, and John C. Hendee. 1971. "Reply to McEvoy: organized conservationists *are* upper-middle class." *Journal of Leisure Research* 3:129–131.

Hendee, John C., Richard P. Gale, and Joseph Harry. 1969. "Conservation, politics, and democracy." *Journal of Soil and Water Conservation* 24:212–215.

Mazur, Allan, and Eugene Rosa. 1974. "Energy and lifestyle." *Science* 186:607–610.

McEvoy, James III. 1972. "The American concern with the environment." In *Social Behavior, Natural Resources and the Environment*, ed. William R. Burch, Jr., Neil H. Cheek, Jr., and Lee Taylor, 214–236. New York: Harper & Row.

McEvoy, James III. 1971. "A comment: conservation an upper-middle class social movement." *Journal of Leisure Research* 3:127–128.

Mitchell, Robert Cameron. 1979. "Silent spring/solid majorities." *Public Opinion* 16:1–20, 55.

Morrison, Denton E. 1976. "Growth, environment, equity and scarcity." *Social Science Quarterly* 57:292–306.

Morrison, Denton E. 1986. "How and why environmental consciousness has trickled down." In *Distributional Conflicts in Environment Resource Policy*, ed. Allan Schnaiberg, Nicholas Watts, and Klaus Zimmerman, 187–220. Aldershot, UK: Gower Publishing Limited.

Van Liere, Kent D., and Riley E. Dunlap. 1980. "The social bases of environmental concern: a review of hypotheses, explanations and empirical evidence." *The Public Opinion Quarterly* 44:181–197.

Public Opinion Trends

Buttel, Frederick H. 1975. "The environmental movement: consensus, conflict, and change." *Journal of Environmental Education* 7:53–63.

Dillman, Don A., and James A. Christenson. 1972. "The public value for pollution control." In *Social Behavior, Natural Resources and the Environment*, ed. William R. Burch, Jr., Neil H. Cheek, Jr., and Lee Taylor, 237–256. New York: Harper & Row.

Gabbard, Anne Y., and C. Milton Coughenour. 1973. "Opinions of Eastern Kentuckians on surface mining and governmental programs." Lexington: University of Kentucky, Department of Sociology RS-34.

Means, Richard L. 1972. "Public opinion and planned changes in social behavior: the ecological crisis." In *Social Behavior, Natural Resources and the Environment*, ed. William R. Burch, Jr., Neil H. Cheek, Jr., and Lee Taylor, 203–213. New York: Harper & Row.

Morrison, Denton E. 1980. "The soft, cutting edge of environmentalism: why and how the appropriate technology notion is changing the movement." *Natural Resources Journal* 2:275–298.

O'Riordan, Timothy. 1971. "Public opinion and environmental quality: a reappraisal." *Environment and Behavior* 3:191–214.

Orr, Robert H. 1974. "The additive and interactive effects of powerlessness and anomie in predicting opposition to pollution control." *Rural Sociology* 39:471–486.

Urban-Industrial Influences

Buttel, Frederick H., and William L. Flinn. 1976. "Environmental politics: the structuring of partisan and ideological cleavages in mass environmental attitudes." *Social Quarterly* 17:477–490.

Catton, William R., Jr. 1980. *Overshoot: The Ecological Basis of Revolutionary Change.* Urbana: University of Illinois Press.

Commoner, Barry. 1977. *The Poverty of Power.* New York: Bantam.

Firey, Walter. 1947. *Land Use in Central Boston.* Cambridge, Massachusetts: Harvard University Press.

Gans, Herbert J. 1962. *The Urban Villagers: Group and Class in the Life of Italian-Americans.* New York: The Free Press.

Gans, Herbert J. 1967. *The Levittowners.* New York: Panthew Books.

Miller, Delbert C. 1972. "The allocation of priorities to urban and environmental problems by powerful leaders and organizations." In *Social Behavior, Natural Resources and the Environment,* ed. William R. Burch, Jr., Neil H. Cheek, Jr., and Lee Taylor, 306–332. New York: Harper & Row.

Molotch, Harvey. 1970. "Oil in Santa Barbara and power in America." *Sociological Inquiry* 40:131–144.

Schnaiberg, Allan. 1980. *The Environment: From Surplus to Scarcity.* New York: Oxford University Press.

Selznick, Phillip. 1949. *TVA and the Grass Roots: a Study in the Sociology of Formal Organization.* Berkeley: University of California Press.

Whyte, William F. 1968. *The Last Landscape.* New York: Doubleday & Co.

Technical Impact

Bertrand, Alvin L., and Harold W. Osborne. 1959. "The impact of industrialization on a rural community." *Journal of Farm Economics* 41:1127–1135.

Breese, Gerald, Russell J. Klingenmeier, Jr., Harold P. Cahill, Jr., and James E. Whelan, et al. 1965. *The Impact of Large Installations on Nearby Areas.* Beverly Hills: Sage Publications.

Burch, William R., Jr., and Donald R. Deluca. 1984. *Measuring the*

Social Impact of Natural Resource Policies. Albuquerque: University of New Mexico Press.

Burdge, Rabel J., and Richard L. Ludtke. 1972. "Social separation among displaced rural families: the case of flood control reservoirs." In *Social Behavior, Natural Resources and the Environment*, ed. William R. Burch, Jr., Neil H. Cheek, Jr., and Lee Taylor, 85–109. New York: Harper & Row.

Buttel, Frederick H., Martin Kenney, and Jack Kloppenburg, Jr. 1985. "From green revolution to biorevolution: some observations on the changing technological bases of economic transportation in the third world." In *Economic Development and Cultural Change*, 31–55. Chicago: University of Chicago Press.

Cottrell, Frederick. 1951. "Death by dieselization: a case study in the reaction to technological change. *American Sociological Review* 16:358–365.

Cottrell, Frederick. 1955. *Energy and Society*. New York: McGraw-Hill Inc.

Field, Donald R. 1968b. *Industrialization and the Rural Community: Local Considerations*. Brookings: South Dakota State University Extension Circular 679.

Finsterbusch, Kurt, and Charles P. Wolf (eds.). 1980. *Methodology of Social Impact Assessment*. Stroudsberg, Pennsylvania: Hutchinson, Ross.

Hertsgaard, T. A., and Larry F. Leistriz. 1973. "Coal development in North Dakota: effects on agriculture and rural communities." *North Dakota Farm Research* 30:7–11.

Hoffer, Charles R., and Walter Freeman. 1955. *A Social Action Resulting from Industrial Development*. East Lansing: Michigan State University Agricultural Experiment Station Bulletin No. 401.

Mumford, Lewis. 1934. *Technics and Civilization*. New York: Harcourt, Brace and World.

Murdock, Steve H. 1979. "The potential role of the ecological framework in impact analysis." *Rural Sociology* 44:543–565.

Thomas, William (ed.). 1956. *Man's Role in Changing the Face of the Earth*. Chicago, University of Chicago Press.

Wolf, C. P. 1986. "Impact ecology: an assessment framework for resource development and management." In *Natural Resources and People: Conceptual Issues in Interdisciplinary Research*, ed. Kenneth A. Dahlberg and John W. Bennett, 231–258. Boulder, Colorado: Westview Press.

Spatial Aspects

Barker, Roger. 1968. *Ecological Psychology.* Stanford, California: Stanford University Press.

Cheek, Neil H., Jr., Donald R. Field, and Rabel J. Burdge. 1976. *Leisure and Recreation Places.* Ann Arbor, Michigan: Ann Arbor Science.

Firey, Walter. 1945. "Sentiment and symbolism as ecological variables." *American Sociological Review* 10:140–148.

Hall, Edward T. 1966. *The Hidden Dimension.* Garden City, New York: Doubleday.

Hodge, Gerald. 1966. "Do villages grow? Some perspectives and predictions." *Rural Sociology* 17:54–70.

Jobes, Patrick C. 1976. "The right to participate: attitudes regarding land use and development in southeastern Montana." In *The Behavioral Basis of Design: Selected Papers,* eds. Peter Suedfeld, James A. Russell, Lawrence M. Ward, Francoise Szigetin, et al., 201–206. Stroudsburg, Pennsylvania: Dowden, Hutchinson and Ross.

Lee, Robert G. 1973. "Social organization and spatial behavior in outdoor recreation." Ph.D. thesis, University of California, Berkeley.

Lynch, Kevin. 1960. *The Image of the City.* Cambridge, Massachusetts: MIT Press.

Michelson, William. 1970. *Man and His Urban Environment.* Reading, Massachusetts: Addison-Wesley Publishing.

Sommer, Robert. 1969. *Personal Space: A Behavioral Basis for Design.* Englewood Cliffs, New Jersey: Prentice-Hall, Inc.

Sommer, Robert. 1970. "The social ecology of a rural community." *Rural Sociology* 35:337–353.

Young, Ruth C., and Olaf Larson. 1970. "The social ecology of a rural community." *Rural Sociology* 35:337–353.

Zeisel, John. 1975. *Sociology and Architectural Design.* New York: Russell Sage Foundation.

Zimmerman, Carle C. 1930. *Farm Trade Centers in Minnesota 1905–1929.* St. Paul: University of Minnesota Agricultural Extension Service Bulletin No. 269.

Zimmerman, Carle C., and Gary W. Moneo. 1971. *The Prairie Community System.* Calgary, Alberta: Agricultural Economics Research Council of Canada.

3

Emergence of Nature as a Partner

Knowledge is cumulative. For a field of inquiry such as natural resource sociology to continue to grow it must take cognizance of the varied intellectual threads that contribute to an understanding of human behavior and the environment. Natural resource sociology draws from many disciplines such as human ecology, anthropology, sociology, biology, and economics. Rural sociology has over the past fifty years, likewise, provided insights into the human behavior-environment equation. All students of human behavior have a basic interest in an encompassing framework where non-human, natural ecosystem variables—soils, nutrients, topography, energy, etc.—become contributing elements partially accounting for observed regularities of human social behavior. Within the practice of rural sociology several theoretical streams have attempted to merge the social with the biological. We believe that these varied frameworks permit the derivation of several principles to guide contemporary theory and method (Figure 7).

During the early years in the study of rural society, as reported in Chapter 1, sociologists were busy documenting the consequences of human actions on the land. Three areas stand out. The first area contains the many studies of agricultural practices, soil fertility and stratification, and studies on the influence of climate and topography on farming at the margins. These studies indicated the close connection between social

Figure 7
Theoretical Streams on Society and Nature in Rural Society

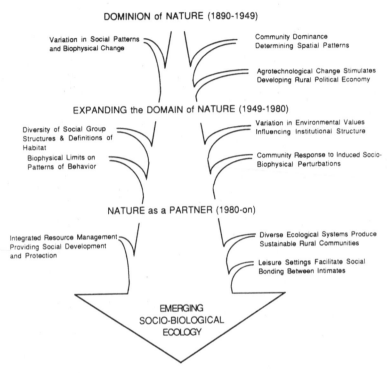

DOMINION of NATURE (1890-1949)

Variation in Social Patterns
and Biophysical Change

Community Dominance
Determining Spatial Patterns

Agrotechnological Change Stimulates
Developing Rural Political Economy

EXPANDING the DOMAIN of NATURE (1949-1980)

Diversity of Social Group
Structures & Definitions of
Habitat

Biophysical Limits on
Patterns of Behavior

Variation in Environmental Values
Influencing Institutional Structure

Community Response to Induced Socio-
Biophysical Perturbations

NATURE as a PARTNER (1980-on)

Integrated Resource Management
Providing Social Development
and Protection

Diverse Ecological Systems Produce
Sustainable Rural Communities

Leisure Settings Facilitate Social
Bonding Between Intimates

EMERGING
SOCIO-BIOLOGICAL
ECOLOGY

patterns and biophysical changes. The second group consists of macro analyses undertaken by scholars of community and small farms who examined agricultural systems, settlement patterns, and population distribution. These studies clarified relations between community dominance and spatial patterns in rural America. The third group of studies is concerned with the development and change within the primary extractive industries—such as agriculture, forestry, and mining. These studies measured such factors as mechanization in agriculture and forestry, the cyclical nature of mining, and the effect of such technological realities on the rural political economy.

We then identified a second period, begun in the 1960s, where the emphasis was less on development and more on the constraining or limiting bounds of nature within which humans must operate. This period of research identified at least four sets of behavioral regularity. The first set identified the most crucial biophysical influences on patterns of social behavior. The second set of findings on rural leisure settings and animal behavior studies illustrated how variations in group structure are associated with variations in definitions of habitats. The third set outlined the work on values and attitudes toward the environment guiding our understanding of variation in environmental values influencing institutional structure and political economy. Finally, the exploration of contemporary energy development and water resource development in particular have documented predictable patterns of community response to induced sociobiophysical perturbations.

These trends in theories, methods, and research findings suggest an emerging conceptual synthesis that we call social ecology, to differentiate it from the urban spatial analyses of traditional human ecology. In the following pages we explore these ideas and outline an agenda for future rural sociological research that blends traditional research issues with new directions on the demands of the 1990s and beyond.

SOCIAL ECOLOGY REVISITED AND REVAMPED

Sociological theory concerns itself with understanding the origins, persistence, alteration, or destruction of a particular pattern or web of social relations. Specifically there is interest in three processes—social bonding (ties between intimates), social integration (linkages among functional elements), and social solidarity (emotional commitment to a larger social whole). Consequently in social ecology we ask questions about the reciprocal influences between natural ecosystem structures and processes, and social system structures and processes. Under what conditions do

1. Natural ecosystem variables serve as a prime, facilitating, or consequent factor in the observed social systems variation?
2. Social system variables influence the natural ecosystem in such a

manner that reciprocal feedback alters the basis of the social system?

Sociological human ecologists have developed a wide range of key metaphors and concepts to delimit the range of observation and analysis. Out of this extended range of issues, attention has generally been given to three common structural and three common processual concepts. Structural properties considered are

1. *Values* as they structure socialization and perception.
2. *Social differentiation*—the universal varieties of age, gender, class, and status that affect the production and distribution of a given political economy's goods and services.
3. *Community*, the aggregated means by which a collectivity develops distinctive and routinized patterns of place and social interaction that distinguish it from similar such aggregates.

Processual elements consider the universal problems of any enduring social system, such as

1. The sustaining of *social bonds* between intimates to ensure survival of individuals.
2. The management of emotional factors such that they sustain *social solidarity* among members of various social units.
3. The *social integration* of functional tasks essential for survival of individuals and the social system.

Conceptually we have outlined these key elements and their flow within a human resource system (Figure 8). The nature of a population, its size, distribution, and demographic configuration, combined with biophysical resource elements, such as soil, water, plants, and animals, are the essential inputs into the system. The adaptive response influences the social relationships (social bonds) that result. Social-bonding mechanisms are structured by a household, kinship, friendship, or other intimate human association's values to create and sustain loyalty toward that association. Such mechanisms also encourage normative performance of age, gender, and status roles that

Figure 8
Key Conceptual Elements of a Human Resource System

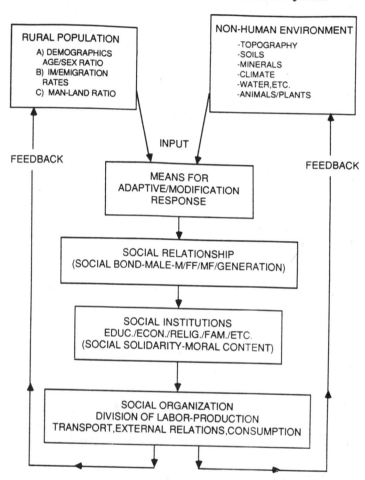

are the basic building blocks of larger, more general associations such as the institutions of a community.

Social solidarity is structured by values that make individuals feel shame, guilt, or pride in their role performance, while rhetoric (finding the available means of persuasion in a given case) is possible and essential because people are apart yet seek symbols to create their unity. At the community level, solidarity is sustained by accepted and ritualized collective explanations of the unexplainable (myth), and thus myth both internally binds and externally differentiates social entities, one from another.

Social integration is structured by shared values regarding necessary roles, patterned and legitimated exchanges between these social roles (and clusters of roles or institutions), and thus the adaptive patterns of the larger society are formed. The social organization of rural society is the result. The dynamic nature of the system is noted where both social and biological change feeds back to the basic building blocks of the system.

Our definition of social ecology uses both the biological and social science tradition. It is the study of the relations between human communities (groups or populations) and their respective environments, especially their physical environments. For the most part, social ecology as practiced in rural sociology has emphasized synecology (relations between communities and their environments) rather than autecology (relations between individual organisms and their environment), which has only recently been considered by psychologists such as Irwin Altman (1975) and Kenneth Craik (1968). The common thread in all such studies is measurement of the "causal" contribution that built or natural environments make to observed social and behavioral patterns. Emphasis is placed on both structure and process.

Further social ecology will give intertrophic exchanges equal importance to our continuing interest in how variations in intercultural, interinstitutional, and interpersonal exchanges affect levels of living, lifestyles, and long-term survival opportunities. For example, studies of nomadic peoples in North Africa (Burch and Cheek, 1974) illustrate how transhumance cycles affect cycles in organizational and symbolic structures. Thus small nuclear kin units are widely scattered in dry periods while large, concentrated tribal units emerge in wet periods. One wonders what transhumance cycle affects the migratory and grouping patterns of the "airstream" nomads in the modern American southwest. Or what are the world consequences as more persons consume grain in the form of beef? On a worldwide basis the American feed-grain connection may prove more harmful than the arms and oil connections.

Social ecological analysis would consider how variations in the forms and amounts of energy affect stability and change in social bonding, social integration, and social solidarity. An excellent example is R. A. Rappaport's (1967) study of the relation between ritual, bioenergetics, warfare, and the symbolic value of pigs in Maring society. Denton Morrison's (1976) study on the equity impacts of various energy supplies and systems is another. Others have explored ways in which one can use time-budget analyses over time (Burch and Burch-Minakan, 1979) and between cultures to see if variations in per capita energy consumption have any significant influence on lifestyle.

Our recommended ecological approach would examine how stability and change in the shape, size, and scope of social hierarchies are affected by resource access, modification, and supply. A good example is D. Gross and B. Underwood's (1971) study of a new sisal plant in a developing country. They trace how fairly equal caloric distributions prior to the establishment of the new factory are soon converted into growing differences between the social classes. And for the working classes, this deficit is likely to produce biological perpetuation of the new class structure; because men now require more calories, their women and children have fewer. The nutritional loss for children at critical periods of development suggest severe mental and physical handicaps for the working class, thereby sustaining or increasing class opportunities from generation to generation. Burch (1976), in a study on air pollution, suggests that the environmental insults in work and residential settings may biophysically sustain existing hierarchial patterns in the United States. Indeed, environmental matters are not the simple concerns of just brown pelicans and peregrine falcons.

Conceptually, social ecology's attention to temporal regularities such as individual and group life cycles, diurnal rhythms, work–non-work cycles, and so forth remains central to ecological analysis. For example, attention has been given to how different kinds of recreationists distribute themselves in space and time, how man-caused forest fires distribute themselves in

space and time, and how boomtowns arise at certain times and
places and decline with equal regularity. Natural resource-
environmental sociology has always given a great deal of attention to how the time-space nexus affects the production of
certain socially desired benefits from combinations of land, labor, and capital. We consider the time budgets of a household
in accomplishing certain tasks, the distance to various fields,
and the distance and time to certain markets, and we attempt
to manage these variables so that the distance covered may be
greater but the rise of certain institutions and technologies
permit a shorter travel time. In recreation studies, we have
examined how religious and social cycles of celebration, holy
days, fasting days, national holidays, and so forth are as fixed
and real as seasonal cycles. We have studied, perhaps overstu-
died, the behavioral regularities associated with sacred spaces
such as wilderness areas and how they are not unlike similar
spaces in residences where mothers and fathers have exclusive
occupancy and places where the whole household regularly
gathers. In wilderness we have sorted by purists and non-pur-
ists, or mode of transportation, primitive or modern. Like the
classic rural sociology studies, environmental sociology documents how the regularities of human use of space and time
map particular social relations, constraints, and opportunities
as clearly as they map biophysical patterns. Intimate and distant social relations, high and low social classes, favored and
despised ethnic, occupational, and caste groupings all have as-
signed and clearly regulated measures as to *when* and *where*
those relations should and should not occur. Consequently,
time and space are not simply physical metrics but are filtered
through a prescribed and predictable cultural metric.

Our studies are less clear empirically, but theoretically suggest that people make trade-offs between time and space. We
see the time spent in a Bangkok traffic jam as a painful cost;
though the distance may be short, the time seems forever. Conversely, the time spent with our lover is a benefit that never
lasts long enough and any distance apart is too great. As the
speed of movement increases, the amount of time we devote to
various activities remains about the same (e.g., journey to
work) though the distance traveled may be much greater. A

poor landless family has a surplus of time, so time costs may be less crucial than distance costs. In contrast, to poor families, wealthier families tend to have more space per capita, have less "free" time, consume more energy per capita, and spend a higher proportion of their incomes on consumption rather than subsistence.

In sum, all human social systems have predictable, routine patterns of time-space dimensions that overlay those of the biophysical. Environmental sociology asks how human time-space dimensions overlay or conflict with the necessary ones of ecosystems. Furthermore, as in ecosystems, environmental sociology notes that there is a third driving force—energy that operates by certain laws of physics and affects human time-space processes. So, too, in human systems, energy—its nature, types, and amounts—greatly affects patterns and processes of time-space factors. We can direct more energy in certain ways and gain more productivity in a smaller space and for a shorter time. We substitute human energy for fossil energy or for renewable energy (such as wind), and each change reflects changes in human organization. A city has a higher per capita fossil energy consumed than a rural village and that is part of the attraction of the city and part of the reason it has a different organizational form. Finally, human social systems have developed an abstraction to try and assign value to energy, time, and space as well as their products—capital. Consequently, each person, household, or community has four regularized measures of their structure and functioning—space, time, energy, and capital. Each can substitute for the other and each can be enfolded into the other.

Table 1 summarizes suggested units of analysis of the time-space dimension and how the four resource budgets are measured and included within a social ecological paradigm. The examples provided here are central tendencies from the literature rather than the specifics of any particular scholar. The point is that there are significant continuities between prior work of applied rural sociology and the work of researchers dedicated to natural resource issues, such as forestry, grazing, mining, recreation, water, energy, and land use.

Table 1
Social Budgets, Units of Analysis, and Illustrative Measures
for Understanding Natural Resource Issues

(Examples only)

	SOCIAL RELATIONS (INDIVIDUAL)	SOCIAL INSTITUTIONS (HOUSEHOLD)	COMMUNITY
TIME	-stage of life cycle -daily/weekly time allocation to various tasks e.g. work, play subsistence	-stage of family life cycle -daily/weekly/ seasonal regularities in time allocation by person to functional tasks	-stage of social evolution -celebration and ritual cycles
SPACE	-personal location of work, play, rest, etc. -property rights in certain personal space/objects	-within residence space allocation e.g. Parents/children -distribution of land ownership amounts, type, etc.	-formal functional spaces, e.g. village square -informal functional spaces, e.g. village well
ENERGY	-Kilocaloric intake-expenditure by certain tasks	-fuel sources by Btu -per capita Btu consumption	-total annual Btu by function -distribution by fuel sources
CAPITAL	-personal income % spent on various functions -non-monetary or inkind income and its expenditure	-total household income -non-monetary resources e.g. garden food -allocation to basic functions	-total village income (taxes and inkind; government subsidy, etc.) -total village expen-ditures by specific function

SOME THOUGHTS ON A SOCIAL ECOLOGY
FOR THE FUTURE

Natural resources sociology has become a significant part of rural sociological studies, theories, methods, and application. Its challenge is to contribute to our understanding of the changing patterns of man and nature in rural regions; to link agricultural systems with resource systems in new patterns of theory and application; and to continue a systematic, but humanistically informed, concern with the moral economy of rural communities.

Although rural sociology has contributed to an ecological

awareness of natural resource systems (first period) and the broadened concept and measurement of nature (second period), the third, emergent vision of social ecology is still being written. In many ways, the stimulus for rethinking traditional approaches to society-nature relations has come from biologists. They are the ones who have raised and often documented the finiteness of world resources and who have sought to link people to all other forms of life.

A variety of social scientists have picked up the lead from the biologists. Lionel Tiger and Robin Fox (1971) have been accused of being wrong headed and "sexist," yet they sought to develop systematic cross-species comparisons. Samuel Klausner (1971) and Burch (1971) may be opaque and confused, but they have sought to incorporate the biological characteristics of humans into classic sociological theories. Roy Rappaport (1967) and A. P. Vayda (1977) may have looked too deeply for functional explanations, yet their studies were the first systematic attempts at including human social processes within ecosystem processes.

Flawed as it may be, E. O. Wilson's *Sociobiology* (1975) remains the major work of this biological look at human society. Wilson may have found too many explanations in genes and too quickly dismissed sociology. Yet his work is the first to offer a truly comparative human ecology. The social scientists could now place their zoological specialization alongside other life forms rather than fumbling with analogies of physics and other mechanical persuasions. P. L. Van den Berghe (1975) is among those from sociology who are reexamining the role of biological variables in sociological analysis.

Of course, like all other species, ours is unique. Our primary mode of adaptation may be culture, which is symbolically communicated. Therefore our social transcript has a potentially infinite persistence and is easier to track than the stories our colleagues tell us about the behavioral pathways of their subject species—wolves, howler monkeys, and the like. Still, this very important and unique adaptive strategy of symbolically transmitted information does not negate the many similarities humans share with other social species.

Indeed, we would argue that all sciences study some form of

the way the natural world is organized. Social ecologists study the ways in which humans organize themselves and how these patterns affect our collective and individual behavior. Such a human ecology is interested in the basic regularities exhibited by all forms of social organization. It uses a comparative approach as the best way to check ignorance. It assumes that certain universal principles can be developed, such that our predictions of the behavioral consequences of certain organizational patterns can include a troop of Japanese macaques, a tribe of Trobriand Islanders, a Hutterite colony, or a contemporary coastal fishing village.

All of these are issues that an interdisciplinary, biologically informed social ecology can meaningfully address. The future could promise much to a field of study willing to overcome its childhood fears of social Darwinism and to leave its protective niche of census tracts and ever more elaborate path analyses. Therefore, we provide a research agenda for the future drawing from the diverse ecological perspectives. The social biological connection is critical for the next step—the examination of the joint interplay of conservation and management of resources essential for a sustainable rural society. Though there will be many paths in the future research agenda, we suggest three promising areas growing out of present trends as a point of departure for discussion and debate. Each will be examined in order.

I. THE ROLE OF LEISURE AND TOURISM SYSTEMS AS STRATEGIES FOR SUSTAINING RURAL SOCIAL RELATIONS

The use of forests as places of refreshment and relaxation is certainly as old as their use for fuel and shelter. Whether in ancient China, Rome, or Wordsworth's England, we find people leaving the cities for holidays in the mountains, hills, and forests. In modern North America, forest-based tourism is often a more substantial income earner than timbering. This is especially so in the arid regions of the U.S. mountain west. For the most part, this income is not part of a major spectacular such as Yellowstone National Park, or part of some large-scale industrial tourism such as Vail or Sun Valley. Rather, it is part of the countless, undifferentiated acres of northern Maine, Michigan, or eastern Oregon where small-scale, locally designed, owned, and operated firms serve tourists visiting the forests for relaxation. The same can be seen in the Gir Forest of India or the Borvilli Reserve outside Bombay. Here, ordinary people from the city come to the countryside to relax and enjoy the rustic atmosphere. The local residents continue to farm, harvest trees, and engage in other forms of primary production. Indeed, that is part of the attraction for the tourists. Most middle-class residents of Bombay have some favored rural area whose hill station they return to year after year. Their actions, like Bostonians in northern Maine, provide substantial income transfer and permit a wiser use of the forest resources because there is supplemental income.

Indeed, in Nepal and other parts of the developing world, as M. Thompson and M. Warburton argue,

if land and wealth are seen as virtually synonymous, and if the population that has to live on the land is increasing rapidly, then we have a negative sum game from which the only possible relief is by way of population stabilization or increased productivity (or both). But, if the equation of and with wealth is severed, closure is no longer inevitable and it is possible (but by no means certain) that the game will become positive sum. (1985:210)

So tourism (and other industries that are not directly landbased), sensitively handled, could result in a quite rapid relaxation of the pressure that the present population increase is placing on the land in general and the forest in particular whilst, in the longer term, it could act so as to stabilize the population itself. (1985:214)

Social scientists have a pathological fascination with work. They seem to ignore the fact that their "natives" spend more time at war, making love, picking lice off one another, gambling, and kicking a ball around a field than they ever devote to utilitarian pursuits. Cheek and Burch (1976) argue that all this research on work tells a good bit about how the division of labor contributes to social integration. However, it does not really contribute to understanding the nature of the social bond, especially between gender and generations, or to understanding the linkages between the basic associations of kinship and friendship to the larger collective representations such as ethnic community or nation-state. They argue that non-work permits the conversion of certain biosocial propensities into symbolic structures that sustain social bonds and link smaller human associations to larger ones.

Therefore we suggest three broad areas of future research on tourism that can build on prior work by natural resource sociology, that have high theoretical value, and that deal with pressing social and ecological issues.

Host-Stranger Relations

Rural areas have long been characterized as closed to outsiders and open to insiders. That is, there is a strong in-group awareness and protectiveness toward strangers from outside the rural community and a high degree of tolerance for eccentricity within the community. As metro centers expand their influence over rural regions enforcing a certain economic and cultural dependence through cash markets, mass media of communication, and improved transportation routes, there will be more frequent host-stranger contacts (Machlis and Burch, 1983). Natural resource sociology in the middle period developed a substantial literature on trends, characteristics, and impacts of wildland recreation. There should be considerable value in applying a transfer of some of the theory and the methods to understanding the sustainability of the emerging small-scale tourist-serving enterprises and their contribution to the economic well-being and cultural sustainability of rural areas. Certainly, like the family farm, "mom-and-pop" enterprises are threatened by the large-scale, chain, tourist enterprises. Furthermore, there is considerable evidence that such absentee-owned enterprises are more subject to boom-bust patterns. So studies of the nature and types, durability, attractiveness, and so forth of small inns, farm tourism, bed-and-breakfast enterprises found in primary production rural areas could be theoretically valuable and of great use in planning the development of primary production regions.

Relations Between Community Elements

One of the most valuable contributions natural resource sociologists have made to the parent discipline is an acute awareness of system interdependence between human society and its ecosystem. The protection of wild places and wildlife and the assurance of plant and animal diversity are seen as essentials for sustaining human life. However, Western solutions such as national parks and wildlife preserves, often have protected world survival values of the world's community of nations at the expense of local rural peoples. Consequently, many national parks and preserves in developing countries are more honored on paper and in national capitals than in the field. The reserves are seen as taking away local life support rather than being of great benefit, because local people and institutions have not participated in the design, management, and benefit of such reserves. The biosphere reserve notion of the United Nations is one approach to resolving these problems (Gregg and McGean, 1985).

However, the program has been organized mostly by physical and life scientists who are primarily concerned with protecting rapidly diminishing resources. Yet, there is a great deal of rhetoric regarding the participation of local people and their need for direct gain from reserves. Indeed, the local people are said to be part of the resource being protected. Again, earlier work done on social institutions and public participation in resource-development projects has easy transferability to the biosphere realm where both protection and development goals are combined. The need for social research is large and urgent.

Relations Between Intimates

Behavior is shaped and influenced by social systems. The social group is the most elementary form of social organization and of critical importance to social bonding among members of society. Identity, self-esteem, values, and attitudes are formed and persist within a group context. Group behavior, over time, develops regularities of action that are observable and distinguishable from individuals who make up the group.

A social group can influence and alter individual action; therefore, different types of social groups display different behavior. Rural sociologists such as Kolb (1921), who studied neighboring patterns, pointed the way, but the natural resource sociologists within the RSS expanded our knowledge of social bonds, groups, and environment. While much of the work emerged within the study of leisure and natural environments, the research models might well be expanded to understand tourism systems and the relationship of activity cycles and population cohorts.

Social environments are created by people in the manner in which they adapt to the biophysical environment and the social meanings shared within those environments. No matter how temporary, a social organization is established by social groups, and this governs the behavior of the people present. Firey (1945) suggests culture and cultural display are key factors in the creation of these social environments. Cultural display such as the language used by occupants, the manner of dress, the technology (i.e., beer bottles and ice cooler, backpacking or other camping gear, or climbing equipment), art forms, and music, to name but a few cultural objects, are all present in recreation environments. Cultural objects and symbolic values attached to places help define appropriate behavior and the kind of people who are welcome. While not the central thrust of the article, W. B. DeVall's (1973) description of mountain climbers in a Yosemite campground, for example, is representative of the conversion of a recreation place into a social environment. Here language and equipment together provide guidance to one's ability to enter and become part of the social world reinforcing the bonds established by a special recreation clientele.

Family reunions in Olympic National Park's Klaloch campground each year likewise reflect the conversion of a recreation place into a social environment where social meanings of family togetherness reinforce the commitment of multiple generations of the same family to one another. The social environment is a family gathering, the campground a backdrop for the activities occurring. Campsites and rules are modified by family members to ensure that a social environment for the family is secured.

R. G. Lee's (1973) description of an ethnic group's definition of a park and subsequent visit hinges on the ability of these people to create a social environment consistent with their values and definition of resources within the park they are visiting. Recent work by R. B. Edgerton (1979) illustrates how some biological-physical environments such as beaches can simultaneously accommodate drug dealing and use, courtship, family activities and picnics, nude bathing, and games of sport. Visitors include blacks, Hispanics, whites, gay families, single-parent families, two-parent families, teenagers, retired adults, and representatives of the baby-boom generation. Social environments for each are established usually without interference from another social environment.

Such perspectives on social environments adapted to the host-guest relationship among tourist sites merits further examination. The Man and Biosphere (MAB) program's research on local communities and equivalent reserves might expand research models to embrace social environments and social-biological habitats as definitional components of MAB areas.

II. THE NATURE AND TYPES OF INTEGRATED REGIONAL RESOURCE MANAGEMENT BEST ADOPTED FOR SUSTAINING RURAL SOCIAL INSTITUTIONS

As we noted in Chapter 2, the work by rural sociologists in third world regions has compelled consideration of practices and projects that did not follow the North American model. A classic approach in this vein was Cottrell's (1955) study that demonstrated the uniqueness of the American opportunity in combining a plethora of resources with values to invest rather than consume. A large number of innovation-diffusion studies were conducted; yet such studies have an individualistic bias and fail to consider undesirable side effects of adopting certain practices such as utilization of pesticides and herbicides. However, a few rural sociologists such as Max Lowdermilk and colleagues (1985) have pioneered work on integrated irrigation systems, and Walter Coward's (1985) community approach to irrigation development has pioneered more sociologically driven applications. Although many of the natural resource sociologists were not aware of such work, they too were examining projects that balanced resource development with community stability.

Both sets of parallel interest were arriving at similar responses to what M. M. Cernea (1985) calls rural sociology's crisis and theoretical vacuum experienced in the 1960s and 1970s. Cernea (1985:14) sees a revitalization of the field with the new focus on a sociology of agriculture.

The concentration on the production process in every agricultural subsector—farming, animal husbandry, forestry, fishing—is a determined move away from the shallow empiricism and theoretical conservatism. As Newby defined it, "the sociology of agriculture, sometimes referred to as the new rural sociology, represents not merely a branch of occupational sociology, but a new approach to rural sociology, one more theoretically informed, holistic, critical and radical than the conventional rural sociology that preceded it.

We believe that this emerging rural sociology has a large place for natural resource sociologists whose biological-ecological perspective is essential for understanding integrated management systems. We outline three likely areas of research concentration.

Resource Cycles Affecting Change and Stability in Rural Institutions

As we noted earlier, there has been substantial research on the influence of resource development projects, and the cycles from start to implementation of those projects, on rural institutions of religion, family, property rights, and gender roles. However, few of these studies have been part of a larger ecological approach that fits human cycles into the larger resource cycles of energy, nutrient, hydrological, climatic, and so forth (Guha, 1985; Fortmann, 1985b). Nor has there been much attention to trade-offs between different resource systems at different points in their life cycle. For example, new varieties of rice are more likely to be tried by poor peasants than new tree species because the period of maturity for trees is much longer. Hence the risk of failure is greater with trees as the farmer cannot make an early correction. Furthermore, different tree species have different cycles and effects from one another, while tree-planning cycles from seed development through planting and harvesting have different cycles than other resource-productive activities such as agriculture, mining, ranching, and tourism. Research on integrated agricultural systems might examine the implication for various rural institutions in combinations of resource cycles for grazing, farming, forestry, and small-scale tourism. For example, the choice of a particular tree species for fuel wood may combine well with certain crops in such a way that surplus time of household members can become productively engaged without distracting from their primary activities. The identification, description, and analysis of such institutional congruence with resource cycles is a valuable field for theoretical and applied research by natural resource sociologists.

Patterns of Adaptation to Change by Human Communities and Rural Institutions

One of the larger research literatures in social science has to do with the factors affecting adjustment to change by human communities. Natural resource sociology has drawn extensively from this literature to examine resource boomtowns and to assess the impact of certain resource policies and actions. An analysis of this literature (Burch and DeLuca, 1984) suggests at least five patterns of adaptation. (1) In some communities a continuity in basic norms permits a smooth transition to changed conditions. For example, E. M. Brunner (1961) reports that the Toba Batak of Sumatra moved from a small, mountain village to a westernized, urban setting with minimum personal and social upset because they retained kinship as the major nexus of interpersonal relationships along with patrilineal descent and traditional life crisis ceremonies. (2)

Some communities have normative systems "primed" to take the induced change. Eskimo transition from dogsled to snowmobile, Plains Indians adoption of horse and rifle, and Maori acceptance of the European sweet potato are examples of communities where norms of hunting or mobility or a particular form of agriculture were "set" for innovations that enhanced existing norms. (3) Changes in the material structure alters the normative structure. For example, a large number of anthropological community studies report that extensive material changes are overshadowed by changes in outlook and social relations (Holmberg and Dobyns, 1962). (4) The more successful adaptations have changes in social norms that precede material changes. A large number of studies illustrate what happens when material changes outrun the normative changes; for example, T. T. Sasaki (1956) describes the failure to transfer modern farm techniques to Navahos because the prevailing norms favored smaller, more subsistence farming. (5) In some communities rapid change, whether material or normative, improvement or decline, produces social fragmentation. The "boomtown" literature spawned by U.S. western energy development provides ample evidence of the need for appropriate timing of changes if severe social disruption is to be avoided.

Our point in this brief overview is to remind us that resource sociology already has a substantial data base that can be adapted to better guide the timing of technology transfer so as to effect the minimum of negative impact on communities. M. W. Hoskins' (1980) example of women rejecting wood from certain fast-growing tree species because it made the food taste like Vaporub deals with social norms regarding taste and smell. Also, Fortmann (1986) summarizes the implications of a wide range of research on sex roles for forestry practices. The large body of community literature in the social sciences could permit anticipation of such responses and provide a substitute base for developing research in the "new rural sociology."

Institutional Change and Stability in Mining and Fishing Communities

Few question the inherent dependence of man on natural resources for human survival. Yet examples of the decline of human population and communities resulting from exploitation of natural resources abound over and throughout the third world and small resource-dependent communities in the developed world (Detomasi and Gartrell, 1984).

Perhaps the plight of small resource-based communities in the United States is not as dramatic as that found in developing societies where resource depletion produces large-scale starvation, but the loss of population and decline of such communities, and the breakup of families are indeed real issues. The technological revolution in the agriculture, forestry, mining, and fisheries industries' fluctuation in the demand for products and the depletion of preferred species results in the growth and decline of the dependent community.

For most rural resource-dependent communities, the economy and occupational structure have been based on a single-species resource such as Douglas fir forest, salmon fisheries, and minerals (silver, gold, and coal). Such communities are less stable and more vulnerable to resource supply availability (Clawson, 1980). The relationship between community structure and resource base requires further attention.

As Landis (1933) and M. Brown and J. N. Webb (1941) point out, resource cycles in the industry alter social conditions of the community. Similarly, fishing communities on the east coast and west coast might be defined as lobster dependent or salmon dependent. As the resource proceeds through biological cycles of growth, decline, and migration, what are the patterns for the human system? Do institutional structures have a definitive contraction-expansion adaptive capability? The concept of stability (perhaps better defined as dynamic equilibrium) for such communities requires more complete operational definition.

Resource-dependent communities are tied to external economic and biological cycles. As nation-states zone the sea, differential extraction processes will leave ecosystems in flux and predator-prey relations unbalanced. As fishery biomass shifts from one preferred species to another, the composition and distribution of the fishing fleet change and their host communities are altered. The dynamics of these social-biological systems remain relatively uncharted. A parallel picture exists for mineral resource communities. As energy demands cycle, the boom-bust cycle of communities follows. The detailed pictures of migration patterns, energy flow, age structure imbalance, and limited occupational structure depict a resource-dependent community in transition. Comparative studies of such communities in various biomes throughout the world might lend insights into logical patterns of resource development and preservation.

III. THE ROLE OF AGROECOLOGY AS A STRATEGY FOR SUSTAINING DIVERSE RURAL COMMUNITIES

Agriculture, forestry, mining, and fisheries practices reflect the general tendencies of our species and the particularities of specific cultural traditions of a given human resource system. As we have noted, the historical pattern for each of these primary production sectors has been exploitation of a preferred species or modification of a biological habitat for a preferred species, with little concern for the interaction effect of one resource activity on another. On the one hand, we have witnessed the decline of the Douglas fir in the Northwest, paralyzing an industry dependent on a single-species forestry practice. Yet the wood biomass available is abundant. The same pattern is occurring in the fishing industry where the decline in salmon is causing an alteration in the composition of the coastal fishing fleet and support communities. Yet in many coastal waters the fishery biomass is abundant. On the other hand, habitats have been altered to accommodate preferred agricultural practices such as the high-grass prairies in Kansas and southern pine forests of Mississippi, with accompanying decline in long-term resource sustainability of the native habitat.

In the coming decades, sustainable rural development will need to move from almost exclusive attention on one resource system—forestry or agriculture or mining or fisheries or tourism—to one that seeks to integrate diverse resource systems. Agroecology, if addressed in a broad perspective, has merit for guiding rural development. But any development program is not an independent action without consequences for other forms of rural resource development. Agriculture is intertwined with the social and economic life of a community—posing simultaneously complementary, competitive, and conflicting demands on the community and its natural resource base. Thus an agroecology system must consider simultaneously: rural people, biotechnology, and biophysical compatibility within a rural region. Three areas of research are suggested that build on an integrated rural resource region.

Biosphere Reserves as Means of Community Development and Integration

Always choices will be made between one form of development action and another. As we look to the twenty-first century, the ecological soundness of rural development remains paramount. In this context, a particular program of rural development simultaneously considering the resource requirements for agriculture development and for fisheries activities, options for forestry, and protection of representative biological habitats has merit. A region that maintains a diverse resource base including a sound fisheries stocking program, regeneration of forests, soil conservation programs for agriculture, and parks and preserves, retains rural development options for the future as well as an attractive resource system for tourism. The ecological interdependency and mutual supporting nature of resource activities must be emphasized over the monocultural resource practices of an earlier time. In this context, biosphere reserves become significant ecological units for resource planning.

Biosphere reserves are potentially important natural resources systems for the world community. Resulting from actions of UNESCO within the United Nations, these reserves represent unique biological habitats that have been established throughout the world. Defined as an area where the diversity and integrity of biotic communities of plants and animals within natural ecosystems are protected, biosphere reserves are set aside for scientific study, the monitoring of ecological change, education, and training (Franklin, 1977). But such places are much more. Scientists as managers of biosphere reserves should recognize that such areas, while defined by the scientific community to be places of conservation and research, often have concurrent designation as hunting, forestry, and agricultural habitats of local and regional populations. The concept of biosphere reserves and indeed the entire Man and Biosphere program implies an understanding of the role of humankind within various ecosystems and the impact of human activity on various ecosystems. Biosphere reserves could become listening posts of ecological change through resource monitoring. Such areas will be more successful when integrated rather than isolated from the human populations in a local area undergoing development programs. When managed in this way, biosphere reserves become "core areas" around which a sociobiological region's diverse resource management regime can be developed. Such reserves are gene pools and partners in sustainable human resource systems. In this way, biosphere reserves can guide rural development rather than be captive to it. Research should be initiated to map the historical and current resource management practices of a region in which a biosphere reserve is established. Assessment of complementary and conflicting resource uses should be identified and then, in the context of a regional community, integrated resource management planning can begin.

Biotechnology in a Sustainable Community Agriculture Perspective

As we approach the future for rural sociology, one overriding conclusion becomes apparent. Rural sociology is the study of the environment, and the emerging ecological framework— within which the diverse studies of foreign and domestic agricultural systems, rural health, community stability, and rural poverty take place—is a prerequisite for understanding the functioning of rural society and the resolution of rural social problems. Agricultural leaders within both business and the land grant institutional structures will benefit from a framework that places agriculture within a rural ecosystem context and supports research accordingly. Too great an emphasis is being placed on biotechnology, genetic research in agriculture and forestry, without due regard to human institutions, human welfare, equity and preservation of rural lands, and rural culture. New plant and animal breeds are being developed, but few agricultural researchers are conducting research on the people who will manage, market, and consume the products (Doyle, 1985). Biotechnology will have a profound influence on man-environment relations. This includes the manipulation of species characteristics, expanding the ecological niche of plants and animals, redefining the meaning of endangered species, and influencing the definition and character of areas set aside as parks and equivalent reserves. Indeed, genetics may become a natural resource soon to be exploited and manipulated as soils, timber, and wildlife have. Yet, we need to ask whether agricultural experiment stations will follow the industrial-commercial mode to compete in the ever increasing genetic energy path or whether such institutions have a moral and practical obligation to explore the question of genetic research for sustainable community agriculture. The cyclical nature of rural problems is striking. The early studies of rural land resources focused on the interrelationship of land tenure systems, farming practices, and soil stability. J. Ashby (1985) illustrates from research in Columbia, that the political economy, including biophysical and institutional factors, creates incentives for farmers to use destructive soil management practices. G. L. Bultena and E. O. Hoiberg (1986), S. B. Lovejoy and T. L. Napier (1986), P. J. Nowak and P. F. Korsching (1983), and others are once again focusing on farming systems and soil erosion in U.S. agriculture and seem to be arriving at the same conclusion Ashby noted. The economic disenfranchisement of many Midwest farmers raises yet another question about land tenure and protection of a land resource.

Finally, the linking of land tenure and intensive farming to soil erosion anticipates contemporary concerns with deforestation in the third world. Ownership and management of land resources have been associated with greater soil stability and use of conservation practices. In third world countries, government ownership of forests removes a key right of the peasant to the land and hence provides little incentive to conserve. Historically, in many countries entering the forest with a plow is the means to claiming ownership.

There is growing research on attention to small-scale diverse agricultural systems, organic farming, and examination of perennials as a basis for a sustaining agricultural production (Jackson, 1980). The focus of the research on biotechnical issues once again links the farmer and community to produce sustainable rural communities. In addition, new products such as rural tourism are emerging as a form of economic development that can complement agriculture and forestry production. If properly designed and at an appropriate scale, tourism may provide the opportunity to sustain rural culture and facilitate social bonding between intimates.

Social-Community Forestry as Systematic Link Between Farm and Community

The range of strategies that have been proposed to develop forest ecosystems for the benefit of local communities seems to be growing at a rate equal to some of the major projections of deforestation rates. Among the many strategies, the following are common: farm forestry that relates to the area around the farmstead; community fuel wood production that is directed to developing rapid-growing species to meet domestic cooking and space-heating needs; silvipasturage, which seeks species that replenish nitrogen for nearby grasses, provide shade for cattle, and produce fodder; small-scale commercial timber and pulp operations; and small-scale nature-based tourism. It is important to note that such programs are directed to local, rural community gain rather than to large-scale overseas export earnings. Furthermore, there is considerable attention to equity factors and ensuring that benefits reach the "poorest of the poor" in rural communities. Social forestry activities have not been part of traditional agriculture or forestry development projects, hence there is a very limited research base on which to develop professional practices of inventory, assessment, monitoring, prescription, and evaluation. Nor are the techniques of involving participation of social units such as households and communities well developed. Again, several strands of natural resource sociology can be brought to bear on such issues—concern with social groups in wildland settings, social impact assessment practices, spatial studies, and the new human ecology theory—and can combine with agricultural and farm systems research emerging in sociology (Cernea, 1985) and anthropology (Rambo and Sajise, 1984) to guide important applied research.

CONCLUSION

Clearly, the social and economic relationships between the agricultural trade center and surrounding region as first depicted by Charles Galpin (1915), in his now classic *The Social Anatomy of an Agricultural Community*, have been superseded. Social and economic ties now link the inhabitants of communities and their surrounding rural regions in America to a larger sphere of social action; indeed, linkage is to the whole world. The early emphasis was on agricultural production and community structure as the dominant form of humankind's manipulation of a natural resource base. Today, attention is given to intensive forestry, energy development, and rural industrialization as competing demands with agriculture for a limited land base. But various aspects—the facts of change, the consequences of it for the social organization of rural life, the interrelationships of community and region, and competition and adaptation of communities of people associated with natural resources—documented by mainstream rural sociologists and the hybrids associated with the Natural Resource Research group have relevancy for understanding adaptation of communities and predicting social change today.

Questions regarding the future of rural sociology's domain will no doubt continue to be posed. There is no way to satisfactorily settle these by decree or fiat. In looking at alternatives, however, it is well to have one's own sense of history in mind. Thus W. H. Friedland (1982) wants to have rural sociology study agriculture alone because he feels that as some separable entity rural society is long since dead in the United States. But how does one realistically separate the production process from those who perform the activity, their kinship groups, and the communities in which they live? Whatever the disciplinary parameters are, or should be, it must include people, human communities, and the resultant relationships of these to the production process and natural resource base. The point holds whether the discipline wants to focus narrowly on the agricultural production process, the use of natural resources located in rural America—forestry, mining, fisheries, and aquaculture as well as agriculture—or the interrelationship of these primary production activities, the people involved, and their implicated communities.

Coming at the problem of parameters from the other side, that is breadth rather than delimitation, R. E. Dunlap and K. E. Martin (1983) argue that rural sociology needs the infusion of "environmental sociology." Yet environmental sociology is a problem focus, not a theoretical orientation. It is doubtful that Dunlap and Martin are suggesting that environmental sociology created ecological theory. Most, if not all, of environmental sociological analysis relies on extant sociological theory or variations of theories of human behavior. Why should we expect otherwise? However, as they strongly argue, an important contribution of environmental sociologists is their willingness to identify and measure the influence of the physical realm, or natural resources, process on human social activity. In short, the contribution of environmental sociology is in the nature of the biological system variables they attempt to incorporate within sociological analysis and their attempts at the measurement or quantification of those natural system variables.

Perhaps early rural sociologists have not received attention or approbation from many environmental sociologists because they couched humankind's adaptation to natural resources mainly within the context of community, the agricultural production process, and change in rural society. Their definitions of resource variables—such as man-land ratios, crop response, and team haul—were proxies for sociobiological variables that today are taken as quantitatively defined, more direct measures, such as amount of rainfall, temperature, acres in wildlife habitat, kilowatts of power, and so on. Still the awareness of significance of the natural environment for human structures is manifest. As Dunlap and Martin (1983) correctly note, man is part of the ecosystem and agricultural production represents human interrelationships with ecosystems, so too is this a connection made by Galpin (1915) Kolb (1921, 1923), Zimmerman (1930), and Carl Taylor, et al. (1955).

Perhaps failure to include early attempts at linking society and ecosystem can also be traceable to the manner of literature within which pertinent analysis was often reported. During the period of 1910 to the mid-1950s, considerable work was undertaken on community and human adaptation to natural resources. Frequently however, it was reported in agricultural experiment station bulletins, cooperative extension service reports, and other forms that comprise the less public, the less well known, the less likely to be cited sources of the typical professional sociologist. One of the unfortunate aspects of rural sociology, as seen by many current practitioners, is the limiting of the range of "relevant" literature to that material appearing either as books or papers in professional journals. In other words, much of the historic analysis in rural sociology appeared in what is now often called fugitive sources.

The difficulty for any emergent field is to blend the diverse literature that serves as its intellectual foundation. The natural resource sociology field is no exception. The environmental sociology literature has drawn heavily from the urban and built environment literature to illustrate the limits of the biological system. In contrast, the rural sociology literature on the environment has had a rural development flavor focusing on the consequence of human manipulation of a natural resource system on social systems.

Both perspectives about natural resources are essential for an evolving field of inquiry. Together mavericks, explorers, and hybrids in the Rural Sociological Society have collectively raised our consciousness about environmental issues and honed the questions we ask about human resource systems. These students of rural society and rural environments have pointed the way toward assessing the complementary or competing resource demands in terms of "sustainable resource management." They have documented the need to view some combination of agriculture, forestry, fisheries, tourism, and parks as an integrated resource system, where resource management leads to a more diverse and sustainable "ecological system." In the future, the plight of the Midwest farmer will be seen as a central issue in natural resource sociology. In the near future, the impact on rural communities of toxic waste disposal, agricultural chemicals, or acid rain will be seen as central issues for rural sociologists. In this future vision, nature truly becomes a partner.

REFERENCES

Social Ecology Revisited

Albrecht, Don E., and Steve H. Murdock. 1984. "Toward a human ecological perspective on part-time farming." *Rural Sociology* 49:389–411.

Albrecht, Don E., and Steve H. Murdock. 1985. "In defense of an ecological analysis of agricultural phenomena: a reply to Swanson and Busch." *Rural Sociology* 50:437–456.

Altman, Irwin. 1975. *The Environment and Social Behavior*. Monterey, California: Brook/Cole.

Burch, William R., Jr. 1971. *Daydreams and Nightmares: A Sociological Essay on the American Environment*. New York: Harper & Row.

Burch, William R., Jr. 1976. "The peregrine falcon and the urban poor: some sociological interpretations." In *Human Ecology: An Environmental Approach*, ed. Peter J. Richerson and James McEvoy III, 308–316. North Scituate, Massachusetts: Duxbury Press.

Burch, William R., Jr. and Laurel Burch-Minakan. 1979. "Time-budget studies and forecasting the social consequences of energy policies—a summary and selected annotations." *Social Science Energy Review* 2.

Burch, William R., Jr., and Neil H. Cheek. 1974. "Social meanings of water: patterns of variation." In *Water and Community Development: Social and Economic Perspectives*, ed. Donald R. Field, J. C. Barron, and B. F. Long, 41–58. Ann Arbor, Michigan: Ann Arbor Science.

Craik, Kenneth. 1968. "The comprehension of the everyday physical environment." *Journal of the American Institute of Planners* 34:29–37.

Gartrell, C. David. 1983. "The social ecology of innovation: a comment to Ashby." *Rural Sociology* 48:661–666.

Geertz, Clifford. 1963. *Agricultural Involution: The Processes of Ecological Change in Indonesia.* Berkeley: University of California Press, Publication for the Association of Asian Studies.

Gilles, Jere. 1980. "Farm size, farm structure, energy, and climate: an alternative ecological analysis of United States agriculture." *Rural Sociology* 45:332–339.

Gross, Daniel R., and Barbara A. Underwood. 1971. "Technological change and caloric costs: sisal agriculture in northeastern Brazil." *American Anthropologist* 73:725–40.

Klausner, Samuel. 1971. *On Man in His Environment.* San Francisco: Jossey-Bass, Inc.

Machlis, Gary E., Donald R. Field, and Fred L. Campbell. 1981. "The human ecology of parks." *Leisure Sciences* 4:195–212.

Morrison, Denton E. 1976. "Growth, environment, equity, and scarcity." *Social Science Quarterly* 57:292–306.

Morrison, Denton E. 1980. "The soft, cutting edge of environmentalism: why and how the appropriate technology notion is changing the movement." *Natural Resources Journal* 2:275–298.

Murdock, Steve H. 1979. "The potential role of the ecological framework in impact analysis." *Rural Sociology* 44:543–565.

Schnaiberg, Allan. 1972. "Environmental sociology and the division of labor." Evanston, Illinois: Northwestern University, Department of Sociology, unpublished paper.

Schnaiberg, Allan. 1980. *The Environment: From Surplus to Scarcity.* New York: Oxford University Press.

Rappaport, Roy A. 1967. *Pigs for the Ancestors.* New Haven, Connecticut: Yale University Press.

Tiger, Lionel, and Robin Fox. 1971. *The Imperial Animal.* New York: Holt, Rinehart and Winston.

Van den Berghe, P. L. 1975. *Man in Society: A Biosocial View.* New York: Elsevier.

Vayda, Andrew P. 1977. "An ecological approach in cultural anthropology." In *Readings in Ecology, Energy and Human Society: Contemporary Perspectives*, ed. William R. Burch, Jr., 3–8. New York: Harper & Row.

Wilson, Edward O. 1975. *Sociobiology: The New Synthesis.* Cambridge, Massachusetts: Harvard University Press.

Strategies for Sustaining Rural Social Relations

Cheek, Neil H., Jr., and William R. Burch, Jr. 1976. *The Social Organization of Leisure in Human Society*. New York: Harper & Row.

Devall, William B. 1973. "The development of leisure social worlds." *Humboldt Journal of Social Relations* 1:53–59.

Edgerton, Robert B. 1979. *Alone Together: Social Order on an Urban Beach*. Berkeley: University of California Press.

Firey, Walter. 1945. "Sentiment and symbolism as ecological variables." *American Sociological Review* 10:140–148.

Gregg, William, and Betsy McGean. 1985. "Biosphere reserves: their history and their promise." *Orion* 4:50–51.

Kolb, J. H. 1921. *Rural Primary Groups: A Study of Agricultural Neighborhoods*. Madison: University of Wisconsin Agricultural Experiment Station Bulletin No. 51.

Lee, Robert A. 1973. "Social organization and spatial behavior in outdoor recreation." Ph.D. dissertation, University of California, Berkeley.

Machlis, Gary E., and William R. Burch, Jr. 1983. "Relations between strangers: cycles of structure and meaning in tourist systems." *Sociological Review* 31:666–692.

Thompson, M., and M. Warburton. 1985. "Knowing where to hit it: a conceptual framework for the sustainable development of the Himalaya." *Mountain Research Development* 5:203–220.

Regional Resource Management Best Adapted for Sustaining Rural Institutions

Bealer, R. C., K. E. Martin, and D. M. Crider. 1982. "Sociological aspects of siting facilities for solid waste disposal: a state-of-the-art study and annotated bibliography." University Park: Pennsylvania State University, Department of Agricultural Economics and Rural Sociology No. 158.

Brown, Malcolm, and John N. Webb (eds.). 1941. *Seven Stranded Coal Towns*, 188. Research Monograph XXIII, Federal Works Agency, Works Projects Administration. Washington, D.C.: U.S. Government Printing Office.

Brunner, Edward M. 1961. "Urbanization and ethnic identity in North Sumatra." *American Anthropologist* 63:508–521.

Burch, William R., Jr., and Donald R. DeLuca. 1984. *Measuring the*

Social Impact of Natural Resource Policies. Albuquerque: University of New Mexico Press.

Buttel, Frederick H. 1982. "Rural resource use and the environment." In *Rural Society in the U.S.: Issues for the 1980s*, ed. Don A. Dillman and Daryl J. Hobbs, 359–372. Boulder, Colorado: Westview Press.

Cernea, Michael M. 1985. "Sociological knowledge for development projects." In *Putting People First: Sociological Variables in Rural Development*, ed. Michael Cernea, 3–21. New York: Oxford University Press.

Clawson, Marion. 1980. "The dying community: the natural resource base." In *The Dying Community*, ed. A. Gallaher, Jr. and Harland Padfield, 55–85. Albuquerque: University of New Mexico Press.

Cottrell, Frederick. 1955. *Energy and Society*. New York: McGraw-Hill Inc.

Coward, Walter E., Jr. 1985. "Technical and social change in currently irrigated regions: rules, roles, and rehabilitation." In *Putting People First: Sociological Variables in Rural Development*, ed. Michael Cernea, 27–51. New York: Oxford University Press.

Detomasi, Don D., and John W. Gartrell. 1984. *Resource Communities: A Decade of Disruption*. Boulder, Colorado: Westview Press.

Elkind-Savatsky, Pamela D. 1986. *Differential Social Impacts of Rural Resource Development*. Boulder, Colorado: Westview Press.

Fortmann, Louise. 1985b. "Seasonal dimensions of rural social organization." *Journal of Development Studies* 21:377–389.

Fortmann, Louise. 1986. "Women in subsistence forestry: cultural myths form a stumbling block." *Journal of Forestry* 84:39–42.

Freeman, David M. 1985. "Middle level organizational linkages in irrigation projects." In *Putting People First: Sociological Variables in Rural Development*, ed. Michael Cerna, 91–118. New York: Oxford University Press.

Gallaher, Art, Jr. and Harland Padfield. 1980. *The Dying Community*. Albuquerque: University of New Mexico Press.

Guha, Ramachandra. 1985. "Scientific forestry and social change in Uttarakhand." *Economic and Political Weekly* 20:1939–1952.

Halcrow, Harold G., Earl O. Heady, and Melvin L. Cotner. 1982. *Soil Conservation Policies, Institutions and Incentives*. Ankeny, Iowa: Soil Conservation Society of America Press.

Holmberg, Allan R., and Henry F. Dobyns. 1962. "The process of accelerating community change." *Human Organization* 21:107–109.

Hoskins, Marilyn W. 1980. "Community forestry depends on women." *Unasylva* 32:27–32.

Krannich, R. 1984. "Personal well-being in rapid growth and stable communities: multiple indicators and contrasting results." *Rural Sociology* 49:541–552.

Landis, Paul H. 1933. *The Growth and Decline of South Dakota Trade Centers 1901–1933*. Brookings: South Dakota State University Agricultural Experiment Station Bulletin No. 279.

Sasaki, Tom T. 1956. "Socio-cultural problems in the introduction of new technologies on Navaho irrigation projects." *Rural Sociology* 21:307–310.

Agroecology as a Strategy for Sustaining Diverse Rural Communities

Ashby, Jacqueline A. 1982. "Technology and ecology: implications for innovation research in peasant agriculture." *Rural Sociology* 47:234–250.

Ashby, Jacqueline A. 1985. "The social ecology of soil erosion in a Columbian farming system." *Rural Sociology* 50:377–396.

Berry, Wendell. 1977. *The Unsettling of America: Culture and Agriculture*. New York: Avon.

Berry, Wendell. 1981. *The Gift of Good Land: Further Essays Cultural and Agricultural*. San Francisco: North Point Press.

Bultena, Gordon L., and Eric O. Hoiberg. 1986. "Voluntarism in conservation behavior: social factors affecting farmers' adoptions of recommended soil conservation practices." In *First National Symposium on Social Science in Resource Management: Program Abstracts*, 184. Corvallis: Oregon State University 86–4, Cooperative Park Studies Unit.

Burch, William R., Jr., and Jerry L. Wade. 1985. "Through the glass darkly: twenty years of natural resource sociology." *The Rural Sociologist* 5:89–95.

Buttel, Frederick H. 1986. "Toward a rural sociology of global resources: social structure, ecology, and Latin American agricultural development." In *Natural Resources and People: Conceptual Issues in Interdisciplinary Research*, ed. K. A. Dahlberg and J. W. Bennett, 129–164. Boulder, Colorado: Westview Press.

Buttel, Frederick H., and Oscar W. Larson III. 1979. "Farm size, structure and energy intensity: an ecological analysis of U.S. agriculture." *Rural Sociology* 44:471–488.

Cernea, Michael M. 1985. "Sociological knowledge for development projects." In *Putting People First: Sociological Variables in Rural Development*, ed. Michael Cernea, pp. 3–21. New York: Oxford University Press.

Doyle, Jack. 1985. *Altered Harvest: Agriculture, Genetics, and the Fate of the World's Food Supply*. New York: Viking Penguin Inc.

Franklin, Jerry. 1977. "The biosphere reserve program in the United States." *Science* 195:262–267.

Jackson, Wes. 1980. *New Roots for Agriculture*. Lincoln: University of Nebraska Press.

Lovejoy, Stephen B., and Ted L. Napier. 1986. *Conserving Soil: Insights from Socioeconomic Research*. Ankeny, Iowa: Soil Conservation Society of America Press.

Lowdermilk, Max, Alan C. Early, and David M. Freeman. 1978. *Farm Irrigation Constraints and Farmer's Responses: Comprehensive Field Survey in Pakistan*. Water Management Technical Report No. 48A-F. Fort Collins, Colorado: Colorado State University.

Nowak, Peter J., and Peter F. Korsching. 1983. "Social and institutional factors affecting the adoption and maintenance of agricultural BMP's." In *Agricultural Management and Water Quality*, ed. F. Schaller and G. Bailey, 349–373. Ames: Iowa State University Press.

Rambo, A. Terry, and Percy E. Sajise. 1984. *An Introduction to Human Ecology Research on Agricultural Systems in Southeast Asia*. Los Banos, Laquana: University of Phillipines.

On the Shoulders of the Future

Dunlap, Riley E., and Kenneth E. Martin. 1983. "Bringing environment into the study of agriculture: observations and suggestions regarding the sociology of agriculture." *Rural Sociology* 48:201–218.

Field, Donald R., and Darryll R. Johnson. 1985. "Rural communities and natural resources: let's not forget the pioneers." In *Rural Sociologists at Work*, ed. B. Bealer, 133–141. University Park, Pennsylvania: The Pennsylvania State University, M. E. John Memorial Lecture Series Fund.

Friedland, William H. 1982. "The end of rural society and the future of rural sociology." *Rural Sociology* 47:489–608.

Galpin, C. J. 1915. *The Social Anatomy of an Agricultural Community*. Madison: University of Wisconsin Agricultural Experiment Station Bulletin No. 34.

Kolb, J. H. 1921. *Rural Primary Groups: A Study of Agricultural Neighborhoods*. Madison: University of Wisconsin Agricultural Experiment Station Bulletin No. 51.

Kolb, J. H. 1923. *Service Relations of Town and Country*. Madison: University of Wisconsin Agricultural Experiment Station Bulletin No. 58.

Taylor, Carl C., Arthur F. Raper, Douglas Enfminger, Margaret J. Haygood, et al. 1955. *Rural Life in the United States*. New York: A. A. Knopf.

Zimmerman, Carle C. 1930. *Farm Trade Centers in Minnesota, 1905–1929*. St. Paul: University of Minnesota Agricultural Experiment Station Bulletin No. 269.

Rural Sociological Society Natural Resources Research Group Chairs (1964–1988)

1964	Wade H. Andrews (Utah State University)
1965	Lee Taylor (Tulane University)
1966	Bruce Byland (Utah State University)
1967	William S. Folkman (U.S. Forest Service)
1968	Lee Taylor (Cornell University)
1969	William R. Burch, Jr. (Yale University)
1970	William R. Burch, Jr. (Yale University)
1971	Neil H. Cheek (National Park Service)
1972	Gordon L. Bultena (Iowa State University)
1973	Rabel J. Burdge (University of Kentucky)
1974	Donald R. Field (National Park Service)
1975	Dean R. Yoesting (Iowa State University)
1976	Ted L. Napier (Ohio State University)
1977	Evan Vlachos (Colorado State University)
1978	Sue Johnson (University of Kentucky)
1979	Riley E. Dunlap (Washington State University)
1980	Frederick H. Buttel (Cornell University)
1981	Thomas Heberlein (University of Wisconsin)
1982	Paul Myers (Bureau of Land Management)

1983   William Freudenburg (Washington State
        University)
1984   Steve H. Murdock (Texas A & M University)
1985   John Carlson (University of Idaho)
1986   Richard Krannich (Utah State University)
1987   Patrick C. Jobes (Montana State University)
1988   Ruth Love (Bonneville Power Administration)

Index

About the Authors

DONALD R. FIELD is currently Associate Dean, College of Agriculture and Life Sciences at the University of Wisconsin. When this book was written he was senior scientist in the National Park Service and Professor in the College of Forestry at Oregon State University. The former Associate Regional Director of Science and Technology and Regional Chief Scientist of the National Park Service in Seattle, he is coauthor of *Leisure and Recreation Places* and coeditor of *Water and Community Development* and *On Interpretation*.

WILLIAM R. BURCH, JR., is the Hixon Professor of Natural Resource Management in Forestry and Environmental Studies and the Institute of Social and Policy Studies at Yale University. He is also Director of the Tropical Resources Institute, a research sociologist with the National Park service, and an affiliate faculty member of the College of the Atlantic. He is the author of *Daydreams and Nightmares: A Sociological Essay on the American Environment*, coauthor of *Measuring the Social Impact of National Resource Policies*, and editor or coeditor of *Social Behavior, Natural Resources and the Environment*; *Beyond Growth—Essays on Nature, Society and Alternative Futures*; and *Readings in Ecology, Energy and Human Society*.

**Recent Titles in
Contributions in Sociology**

Five Scenarios for the Year 2000
Franco Ferrarotti

Uniforms and Nonuniforms: Communication Through
Clothing
Nathan Joseph

Housing Markets and Policies under Fiscal Austerity
Willem van Vliet—, editor

Religious Sociology: Interfaces and Boundaries
William H. Swatos, Jr., editor

Bureaucracy Against Democracy and Socialism
*Ronald M. Glassman, William H. Swatos, Jr., and Paul L.
Rosen, editors*

Housing and Neighborhoods: Theoretical and Empirical
Contributions
*Willem van Vliet—, Harvey Choldin, William Michelson, and
David Popenoe, editors*

The Mythmakers: Intellectuals and the Intelligentsia in
Perspective
Raj P. Mohan, editor

The Organization-Society Nexus: A Critical Review of
Models and Metaphors
Ronald Corwin

The Concept of Social Structure
Douglas V. Porpora

Emile Durkheim: Ethics and the Sociology of Morals
Robert T. Hall

The Development of a Postmodern Self: A Computer-Assisted
Comparative Analysis of Personal Documents
Michael Wood and Louis Zurcher

The End of Conversation: The Impact of Mass Media on
Modern Society
Franco Ferrarotti